NEWTOWNARDS
IN THE GREAT WAR

NEWTOWNARDS IN THE GREAT WAR

LINDSAY ALLISTER

Pen & Sword
MILITARY

Thank you to the Somme Centre in Newtownards and the families of North Down for donating so many beautiful photos for this book.

First published in Great Britain in 2019 by
PEN & SWORD MILITARY
An imprint of
Pen & Sword Books Ltd
Yorkshire – Philadelphia

Copyright © Lindsay Allister, 2019

ISBN 978 1 78383 200 2

The right of Lindsay Allister to be identified as Author of this work has been asserted by her in accordance with the Copyright, Designs and Patents Act 1988.

Printed and bound in England

by CPI Group (UK) Ltd, Croydon, CR0 4YY

Typeset in Times New Roman by SRJ Info Jnana System Pvt Ltd.

Pen & Sword Books Limited incorporates the Imprints of
Atlas, Archaeology, Aviation, Discovery, Family History, Fiction, History, Maritime, Military, Military Classics, Politics, Select, Transport, True Crime, Air World, Frontline Publishing, Leo Cooper, Remember When, Seaforth Publishing, The Praetorian Press, Wharncliffe Local History, Wharncliffe Transport, Wharncliffe True Crime and White Owl.

For a complete list of Pen & Sword titles please contact
PEN & SWORD BOOKS LIMITED
47 Church Street, Barnsley, South Yorkshire, S70 2AS, England
E-mail: enquiries@pen-and-sword.co.uk
Website: www.pen-and-sword.co.uk
Or
PEN & SWORD BOOKS LIMITED
1950 Lawrence Rd, Havertown, PA 19083, USA
E-mail: Uspen-and-sword@casematepublishers.com
Website: www.penandswordbooks.com

Contents

Introduction   1

Chapter One   1914: Eager for a Fight   7

Chapter Two   1915: Deepening the Conflict   49

Chapter Three 1916: The Realization   74

Chapter Four   1917: Seeing it Through   94

Chapter Five   1918: The Final Blows   115

Index   137

Introduction

During recent years many people have become interested in Newtownards and the surrounding area in County Down, Northern Ireland. As it is one of the bigger towns outside of Belfast, it has a diverse history that can provide a snapshot of what has happened in the rest of Ireland at any point in history.

The history of Newtownards stretches back to the first hunter-gatherers who settled in the area around Scrabo Hill and Strangford Lough. During the Neolithic period, around 3500 to 2000BC, the first farmers grew crops on the rich volcanic soils around Scrabo Hill. A small village was established on Scrabo Hill between 2000 and 300BC, during the Bronze Age, and is believed to be one of the best-known Bronze Age settlements in Ireland. During this period a huge fort stood on the top of Scrabo Hill. A few miles away from the hill, on what would become the east of the town, a monastery was founded in 540AD by Finnian. Movilla Abbey became a holy place in the kingdom of Ui Blathmac. It is believed that Finnian brought the first Bible to Ireland and it was kept in Movilla Abbey. This ancient kingdom saw its share of bloodshed, and the abbey at Movilla was burned and destroyed repeatedly over the years. The ruins of the abbey still stand today and mark the boundary of the town graveyard, a place where many of the fallen soldiers from the Great War were laid to rest.

The town as it is known today would not appear until Hugh Montgomery came and rebuilt the ruins. The town had been left destroyed from Viking attacks; it was a shell with very few people still living in the area. Montgomery began rebuilding in 1606 after winning the favour of King James. Since then, the area has grown into one of the busiest places in Ulster, apart from Belfast.

Before the Great War began, the area had a diverse trade. Newtownards was a large market town, although the biggest

Victoria Square, Belfast.

Linenhall Street, Belfast.

Bedford Street, Belfast, 1917.

Killynether House is found just outside Newtownards at Scrabo Hill.

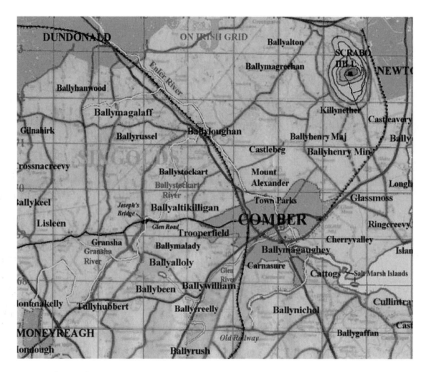

Map of Comber.

Laurel Bank FC Comber football team, 1912.

Victoria Avenue, Newtownards.

town in County Down was Newry. In Ballygowan and in the small townlands, the women produced beautiful embroidery to be sold at market. Most of the flax-making in the area could be found in Comber, as well as Comber Whiskey and the humble (but popular) 'Comber spuds' (new potatoes). Greyabbey and Donaghadee were popular seaport towns where people from Belfast came to holiday during the summer. Throughout the Ards area, farming was one of the biggest sources of employment. Despite the different types of employment, young men still chose to move away to America and Australia to make their fortunes. Many families had three children or more, but a few families were very large with ten or more children. At the time of the 1911 census, Newtownards was a Unionist town with a population of 9,587 people and was about to become the centre of one of the biggest political changes of the twentieth century.

Newtownards Railway Station.

The Most Appalling Disaster in Maritime History.
The White Star Liner "TITANIC," sunk on her maiden voyage off Cape Race, 15th April, 1912.

The 'unsinkable ship', RMS Titanic.

CHAPTER ONE

1914: Eager for a Fight

To many people, including those who lived there, Newtownards was just a normal town in a normal rural area in the north of Ireland. However, in the town and the surrounding area people were preparing to fight and the entire country was on the brink of social discord. It was at this point in Ireland's history that civil war was on the verge of breaking out. The decision for Ireland to stay in the Union with Scotland, England and Wales was slowly creeping out from the hands of the politicians and into the hands of armed civilian forces.

Ireland is divided into four provinces: Ulster, Munster, Leinster and Connacht. There was once a fifth province named Meath but it was divided between Ulster and Leinster at some point before the Norman invasion. By the 1900s, these provinces served no political purpose but showed the remaining divisions that once separated Ireland into different kingdoms of the Celtic lords. The largely Unionist area of Ulster in the north of Ireland was preparing to take up arms in order to remain part of Britain. The other three territories had grown tired of British rule in the country and were considering taking action to separate from the Union. Civil unrest was beginning to stir as the threat of Home Rule hung over people's heads like a guillotine, challenging everyone's way of life. The area of County Down in Ulster was mainly a Unionist population of both Protestants and Catholics, and neither side of the religious population could see any merit in Home Rule. This may seem strange with the popular belief being that it was Catholics versus Protestants in the Home Rule debate, but that is a common misconception. The Unionist population was mainly Protestant but not exclusively. At the beginning of 1914

Postcard showing what people believed Home Rule would look like in Bangor.

the religious persuasion of the town was noted and published in the *Farmers' Almanac* for the year. There were 2,333 Protestant Episcopalians, 5,381 Presbyterians and 623 Methodists living in the town. The resident Catholic population was significantly smaller at 885 people and 365 people had registered themselves as being part of another religious denomination. A person's religious beliefs had nothing to do with their belief in Unionism and anything that threatened the union between Britain and Ireland was seen as treason against the Crown. One of the main reasons for this loyalty was the heritage of the people who lived there. Many of the families who lived in Newtownards were descended from Scottish or English immigrants. Other families around the north coast were descended from Spanish sailors. These sailors had been washed ashore after the ships crashed around the north coast during the Battle of the Spanish Armada in 1588. Many of these families had been settled here for more than 200 years but did not forget their roots or their allegiance to the Crown. The people of the north had a diverse cultural history, unlike many families in the rest of

DONEGALL PLACE, BELFAST, UNDER HOME RULE.

COPYRIGHT.

BAIRD, BELFAST.

Carrickfergus Castle, under Home Rule

the country who were mainly Irish descendants, and some of these families claimed that they could trace their family tree back to the time of the clans.

What was Home Rule?

From the 1870s until after the Great War, the Home Rule debate was at the forefront of Irish politics. From the 1880s onwards, the people of Ulster were determined to be seen as British and cast off many of the superstitions that surrounded them. The first Home Rule Act was foiled in a surprise twist. The opponents to Home Rule claimed that most of the population of Ireland believed in fairy folk and that superstitions clouded people's judgement. It was believed by many politicians that the belief in superstitions was so strong it had got to the point of causing the deaths of children. This surprise accusation during the debates fuelled the belief that the people of Ireland could not be trusted to govern themselves. The argument was put forward that in some of the more rural areas families were alone and isolated, which was detrimental

Ulster's
Solemn League and Covenant.

Being convinced in our consciences that Home Rule would be disastrous to the material well-being of Ulster as well as of the whole of Ireland, subversive of our civil and religious freedom, destructive of our citizenship and perilous to the unity of the Empire, we, whose names are under-written, men of Ulster, loyal subjects of His Gracious Majesty King George V., humbly relying on the God whom our fathers in days of stress and trial confidently trusted, do hereby pledge ourselves in solemn Covenant throughout this our time of threatened calamity to stand by one another in defending for ourselves and our children our cherished position of equal citizen-ship in the United Kingdom and in using all means which may be found necessary to defeat the present conspiracy to set up a Home Rule Parliament in Ireland. ¶ And in the event of such a Parliament being forced upon us we further solemnly and mutually pledge ourselves to refuse to recognise its authority. ¶ In sure confidence that God will defend the right we hereto subscribe our names. ¶ And further, we individually declare that we have not already signed this Covenant.

The above was signed by me at_____
"Ulster Day," Saturday, 28th September, 1912.

God Save the King.

Ulster's Solemn League and Covenant.

to their wellbeing. This isolation was so bad in some places that they were cut off from regular contact with other people and it was this isolation that allowed superstitious beliefs to play havoc with their judgement. In the past it had been reported that some people believed that their children were stolen during the night and a 'changeling' or fairy had taken their place. However, these fairy folk of rural Ireland were not the beautiful winged creatures that many would imagine. Instead they were evil, magical creatures that could destroy families. In order to rid their homes of these evil creatures, the people turned to the myths and legends that had been passed down through the generations. The most popular and efficient method of killing the creatures was to use fire and many children were burned alive as a result. It is impossible to know the exact figures of how many children were killed in this way, but it is believed that the Unionists inflated the figure to suit themselves. It is entirely possible that the claims of burning children were completely made up by Unionists as a way of belittling the Irish.

The third Home Rule Act (Government of Ireland Act 1914) was passed in the House of Commons but later defeated in the House of Lords in Westminster. The previous Bills had been treated in the same way and it was never implemented. It would not be until after the Great War was over that the third Home Rule Act was eventually succeeded by the Government of Ireland Act 1920. This Act separated the north and south of Ireland and it remains this way to the present day. The Home Rule Act was intended to give Ireland back to the people as a republic. No longer would the people of Ireland live under the rule of the Crown and British Parliament; they would be free and independent to govern themselves. However, although most of Ireland craved this freedom, the people of the north of the country feared for their freedom if it was implemented. Simple choices that they had taken for granted would have been stripped away. The Catholic Church had decreed that families of mixed-religion marriages would be forced to raise their children as Catholics rather than having a choice regarding their children's religion. To many people 'Home Rule means Rome Rule' and this became the slogan for their action.

From the very start of 1914, people began taking action against the potential victory of the Act of 1914. A huge petition was put to King George V in January 1914, signed by thousands of

His Grace the Duke of Abercorn, K.G. President of the
Ulster Unionist Council, signing the Solemn League and
Covenant, on Ulster Day 1912, at Baronscourt Co. Tyrone.
Copyright Photo by W. R. Henderson

The Duke of Abercorn, KG, President of the Ulster Unionist Council,
signing the Solemn League and Covenant on Ulster Day 1912.

working men against Home Rule. The local paper, the *Newtownards Chronicle*, reported the petition and stated:

> The 'people' say: The Hon Secretary of the National Workmen's Council have just conveyed to the Home Office a large petition, signed by thousands of working men throughout the country, for presentation to the King. It prays his Majesty to withhold the Royal assents to the Home Rule Bill until the elections of the country have been consulted. This is the first memorial sent to the King against Home Rule.

People did not think that the Home Rule Bill would be passed as the previous Bills had been turned down. However, as most of the country was craving the need for independence from Britain, an anger was stirring in the south of the country at being denied the right to rule themselves. The people of Ulster knew this and they were determined to take any steps to ensure that they were also heard and to show the government that they meant business.

INSPECTION BY SIR EDWARD CARSON OF THE DONEGAL VOLUNTEER REGIMENT, RAPHOE, OCTOBER 2ND, 1913.

UVF inspections.

The Ulster Volunteer Force

The local Ulster Volunteer Force (UVF) had begun its own resistance in the face of Home Rule. The Volunteers were sanctioned and approved by Sir Edward Carson, a Unionist politician and barrister who was campaigning to ensure that Ireland remained British. Carson had become the leader of Ulster Unionism in February 1910 but had been an Orangeman since he was a teenager. He was considered one of the greatest lawyers in Irish history with a string of high-profile cases under his belt. He was the solicitor who was responsible for ruining the poet and playwright Oscar Wilde in the late 1890s. Carson and Wilde had known each other during their time at Trinity College in Dublin. When Wilde heard that the Marquess of Queensberry had engaged Carson's services over claims of homosexual activity and slander, Wilde reportedly said that Carson would 'pursue his case with all added bitterness of an old friend', which he did. Carson proved that Wilde was engaged in homosexual activity, which was illegal at the time, and that Wilde's case of libel against Queensberry was false. The cross-examination from Carson resulted in Wilde being prosecuted for gross indecency. After two years of hard labour, Wilde moved to France where he died penniless in 1900. If this was what Carson was capable of against an old friend, he would definitely pose a problem for those he didn't like. The Unionist population knew all about the Oscar Wilde case and Carson's reputation for being ruthless when it came to the courtroom and matters of the law. They believed that he

Sir Edward Carson.

Edward Carson.

would take the same approach when it came to the Home Rule Crisis with the passion that only a member of the Orange Lodge could.

The units of the UVF consisted of local men who volunteered their services and their lives to protect Ulster. When rebel groups form, they tend to be a group of disorganized youths who have nothing better to do than cause disruption. These men were nothing of the sort and they were far from being the disorganized group of rebels that one might imagine. The men who enlisted were from all walks of life, from highly-paid professionals down to the average working man. There were also plenty of former military men who joined the cause and provided training in many different areas of warfare. Some of these men were previously high-ranking soldiers who turned the units of men into highly-organized and well-trained soldiers. Training was held on a regular basis using wooden or dummy rifles in place of the real thing. This caused quite a bit of mockery from the Nationalist forces and non-Unionists. Newspapers around Britain and Ireland openly mocked the Volunteers and provided plenty of jokes at their expense. Despite the jokes about the dummy rifles, the idea and the method behind them proved to be efficient. The idea of using dummy guns for training would be adopted by the Home Guard nearly thirty years later in 1940 when they used brush shafts instead of guns, and this would be considered a crude imitation of how the Volunteers had trained. Unlike the Home Guard, the Volunteers shaped the wood as close to a rifle as it could be, using pitch pine or spruce. Some of the dummy guns had bolts and nails to help the volunteers practise bolt operation and pulling a trigger. This allowed the Volunteers to become familiar with handling a rifle without ever holding one. When the Volunteers finally received guns of their own, the weight and feel of the dummy rifles made handling a real rifle feel like second nature to them.

As well as the army standard of training, the Volunteers incorporated many other aspects of the army into the UVF. Armlets were issued to every member of the force in order to show rank. Each armlet contained the battalion number, the letters 'UVF' and the name of the regiment. Just like the British army, they had inspections and marched publicly through towns to show their strength in the face of resistance. When Volunteers had completed a certain number of drills and had an excellent attendance record, they were issued with lapel badges. At one point in 1913, the badges were being issued at a great rate with nearly 10,000 Volunteers a week receiving one.

During January 1914, Sir Edward Carson inspected the local Newtownards UVF and gave the troops a glowing report. Carson was impressed by the numbers and the level of discipline shown by the men. Within a few short years of the UVF conception, it had become a private army for the war on Nationalism. Despite not having any guns or firepower, the manpower behind the force began to ruffle some people's feathers. During this time, after the mockery from the press over the dummy guns, Carson was advised to bring a mass amount of weapons into Ulster. The UVF had a small number of weapons that had been smuggled in over the previous years but the surge in manpower meant that many

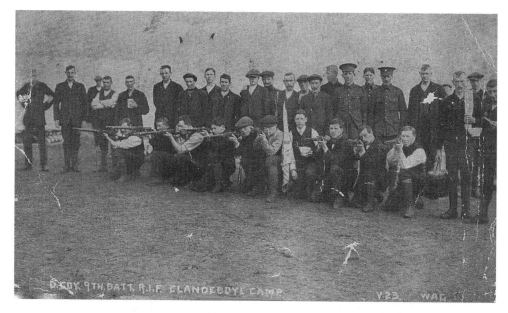

The UVF training.

Volunteers went unarmed. Bayonets were issued to every man and some were stamped with official UVF markings. Those in command believed that every man should carry a bayonet in case ammunition ran out during a blockade or extended fighting.

On 24 February, Edward Carson was forced to place a notice in the local papers after false rumours of the Volunteers' intentions were circulating through the country. The notice stated:

> Rumours have been sedulously circulated to the effect that the Ulster Volunteer Force has been organised with an object hostile to those of our fellow countrymen in Ulster who differ from us. I desire that it should be made plain on all occasions that it is the sole object of the Ulster Volunteer Force to make it impossible for the Government to compel us to submit to a Home Rule Parliament in Dublin.
>
> Our quarrel is with the Government alone, and we desire that the religious and political views of our opponents should be everywhere respected. We fight for equal

Marching through Belfast, 1914.

Marching in Newtownards. Scrabo Tower can be seen in the distance.

Comber UVF, 1914.

justice for all under the Government of the United Kingdom.

Edward Carson, 24 February 1914.

People believed that the force was shaping into a private army that was going to be used against the ordinary people. The training and the small increase of weapons meant that people outside the Unionist forces began to see the Volunteers as a threat. The purpose of the force was to prevent the Home Rule being implemented in Ulster, but some took this to mean that the ordinary people would be a target for terrorism. Rumours had begun to circulate that the UVF would be used against anyone who opposed their political agenda, not just the British and Irish governments.

The praise for the UVF did not end with Edward Carson's first inspection of the year. On 26 February 1914, the local unionist

The UVF at Clandeboye camp.

club publicly acknowledged the Volunteers as a Unionist military organization and as a form of defence for the people of Ulster. It was hoped that the mere threat of violence against Home Rule would be enough to change the minds of those who would impose it. However, within the ranks of the UVF some of the higher officers began to grow frustrated by the lack of weapons for the volunteers. After Carson had sanctioned the action to bring more weapons into Ulster, the officers began tracking down ways to make it happen.

The first official inspection of the Newtownards Volunteers took place at the rear of the spinning mills at Castle Gardens under a stormy sky. The rain fell as the units of the Newtownards District were inspected by Lord Dunleath, the battalion commander, and Colonel Sharman-Crawford. There were two sections of the UVF from Newtownards and two from Comber, one from Donaghadee and Ballywalter. These were the men who were considered to be the force that would break Home Rule. The men marched proudly through the town to Conway Square in the town centre with the Union Jack flying. When they reached the town square they were dismissed. The *Newtownards Chronicle* reported the joy and admiration for the men from the people of the town as they watched the Volunteers parade past them and through the streets. The paper printed a poem along with the story in commemoration of the event. For the local UVF man, this parade would make it a day to remember:

> But when we tread the slushy streets,
>
> And march into the Square,
>
> Their fears die out, their hopes arise,
>
> In answer to their prayer.

> Oh may we prove a guard indeed,
>
> Still worthy of the name;
>
> To hold the pass through years to come,
>
> And spoil the traitor's game.

Local man goes missing

Although the town was consumed with the actions of the local Volunteers and the subject of Home Rule, other things were still

The UVF at Clandeboye camp.

happening. The small population of the area meant that most people knew each other and tended to look out for one another. On 10 January, people were alerted to the disappearance of a local man named Andrew Lockhart who was an employee of the Clandeboye Estate in Bangor. He was last seen in Conlig, a small village that lay between Newtownards and Bangor. He was visiting a friend in the evening before disappearing without a trace. What struck his friends as strange were his parting words to them, as he told them that he would never see them again. A manhunt was mounted and everyone was asked to keep an eye out for him. His final words to his friends sparked rumours that he was unwell in his mind and might be a bit dangerous. His body was found nearly a month later in a lake in Bangor when someone discovered it by accident. The official ruling regarding his death was accidental drowning, but people believed that he had killed himself by jumping in the lake. No one was sure why he would have killed himself or how it happened. The court had ruled that he had probably fallen into the lake when he was walking home in the dark and nobody really wanted to believe that he had taken his own life.

Colonel Crawford (left) with arms dealer Benny Spiro March 1914

Major Crawford and Benny Spiro.

Gun-running

On 24 April 1914, the men of the Ulster Volunteer Force from Newtownards and the surrounding areas began a large-scale gun-running operation. This was in order to arm themselves in the event of an uprising or attack. Up until December 1913 it had been easy to bring guns into the country, but a Royal Proclamation had then made it illegal to bring in military weapons. Once the proclamation had been made, the various forces were ordered to be on high alert for suspicious activity around the docks and ports. Arms had been smuggled into Ireland on a number of occasions but the scale was small and barely noticeable.

Frustrated by having so little to show for so much work, Major Frederick Crawford – Director of Ordnance of the UVF – pushed for a large-scale operation to bring the weapons that the Volunteers badly needed into the country. Crawford was a devout Unionist and was so greatly opposed to Home Rule that he was prepared to arm himself and others to fight against it. His previous plans to bring arms into the country had worked so well that when he suggested the large-scale operation the Ulster Unionists could hardly object. An operation in June 1913 had gone badly when the police found a storage warehouse that contained more than 7,000 rifles. After this, Crawford made little or no attempt to hide the fact that he was bringing guns into the country. He knew that customs officers would see them and try to take them, but the message behind this was clear. The UVF would be armed and there was nothing the government could do to stop the weapons coming. When weapons were seized it made the Volunteers more determined to get them past customs. With the support of the Ulster Unionist Council and the Volunteers, Crawford pushed for a massive import of weapons.

The weapons had been purchased in Hamburg, Germany from an arms dealer named Benny Spiro in early 1914 by Major Crawford. It was believed that he purchased 20,000 rifles and more than 2,000,000 rounds of ammunition, although rumours have put the number of rifles as high as 50,000. Crawford then secured the use of the SS *Fanny* to ship the weapons on 30 March from Germany to Ireland. While the ship was transporting this vast amount of armoury, it was nearly seized by Danish customs. They believed that the weapons were for the Icelandic militants and not heading to Ireland. Their cover was blown and the ship managed to escape in a gale towards Britain. Crawford realized that the ship would probably be seized off the coast now that the Danish authorities had discovered the weapons. While the SS *Fanny* was still at sea, Crawford bought another vessel in Glasgow called the

SS *Clyde Valley* and made a switch. The entire cargo of the SS *Fanny* was transferred to the SS *Clyde Valley* while they sat off the coast of County Wexford. To completely conceal the identity of the ship, her name was changed. Large canvas strips were strung on the outside, covering the name of the *Clyde Valley*. However, a ship with no name would look suspicious heading into Belfast Lough so they renamed the boat for one night as *Mountjoy II*. This name was in remembrance of the armed merchant ship that broke the boom on the River Foyle and brought much-needed supplies during the Siege of Derry in 1689.

All the planning was to pay off on 24 April. Across Ulster, the Volunteers were told they needed to take place in a test mobilization of the Motor Corps. The men from Newtownards marched from the town centre to Donaghadee, believing that they were about to take part in a drill as nobody had been told of the plan. Only a few people knew what was really happening and this secret was kept within the higher ranks. By 10.00 pm, the pier at Donaghadee was beginning to fill with men and motor cars. One man, a coastguard named H.E. Paynter, had been one of the first men to realize what was happening. He rushed to his commanding officer, Lieutenant Commander Gerald Ducat, to inform him what was happening at the pier. When Paynter arrived at the home of Ducat, the house was empty. Ducat did not return home until around 1.00 am when he found the body of Paynter lying at his front door. In his rush to tell his commanding officer, Paynter had suffered a heart attack, collapsed in the doorway of Ducat's home and died. The police and the coastguard appeared to investigate what was happening but the Volunteers blocked their path and would not let them through. The police and coastguard had been made aware that there was possibly a shipment of weapons attempting to land after the boat had been discovered by the Danish authorities. *The Times* newspaper had reported the story of the ship carrying weapons and had guessed that she was heading to Ireland. Despite this knowledge, the police and coastguard did not have the manpower in the area to prevent the ship landing and they were greatly outnumbered. To ensure that no one could raise the alarm and send reinforcements, telephone and telegraph connections were cut.

Meanwhile, out in Belfast Lough, a ship named the SS *Balmerino* was acting suspiciously as she travelled down the lough.

A drawing showing the gun-running by the UVF in 1914.

The coastguard was dispatched into the water to prevent the ship from landing as they believed that this was the ship that carried the guns. They surrounded the vessel and stopped her in her tracks, not realizing it was a decoy that had been loaded with coal. While the coastguard was busy with the search and capture of the SS *Balmerino*, the SS *Mountjoy II* sailed past into Larne harbour to meet up with two other vessels. In the dark waters of the lough they began to unload the weapons into two other boats. The SS *Innis Murray* was loaded up and sent to Donaghadee where the Newtownards Volunteers were waiting. At 2.00 am Lord Dunleath arrived at the pier to ensure that everything was going smoothly. Although the police and other officials were there, they had been cordoned off by a group of men and were not allowed to move. Lord Dunleath refused to allow them to leave and ordered men to watch them until the task was finished. If the officers had been allowed to leave they could have called for help and the operation would have been in vain. At 3.00 am the last few motor cars and men arrived and everything was ready to begin taking the shipment off the boat. The *Innis Murray* was not sighted off the pier until 5.30 am but by 6.00 am she had docked and began unloading her

The UVF marching.

precious cargo. The cars that had the longest distance to travel were loaded with their cargo first, those with the shortest distance received their goods last, and the Newtownards Volunteers were the very last to receive their weapons. Within three hours the Volunteers had emptied the boat and the weapons were being spread across the country. Safe houses across County Down had been set up months before for the storage of any weapons and gear for the Volunteers. Many high-profile residents of Newtownards were rumoured to have taken in and stored guns. It was rumoured that some of the weapons were stored at the home of the Mayne family at Mount Pleasant Estate in Newtownards but this was not confirmed until the house was being renovated years later. The Mayne family were land and business owners in the town and the family had lived on the estate since 1820. It is clear that the call to defend the country pulled in many different types of people. The British army, which was stationed in the area, did not hear about the gun-running until a few hours after the men had left the pier and the officials who were cordoned off had been released. By this time it was too late for the British forces to do anything about it as there was no trace of the operation that had taken place.

The beginning of July marked the start of the July celebrations. The date of 1 July is the anniversary of the Battle of the Boyne and the victory of William of Orange. Every year the town would come alive with parades and marching bands. On 12 July every year, the Orangemen of Ulster joined together to march through the streets. Bands played drums and pipes, flutes filled the air and banners were held high as part of Orange Pride. Every man, woman and

King George and his cousin.

child went to the streets to watch the men march and listen to the music from the marching bands. For one day, the country forgot that it was at war with itself. The celebrations were partially joyful this year after the success of the gun-running. The town was filled with joy and celebration as the great tradition of the Orange Order was honoured for another year by everyone who lived in the town.

The outbreak of war

On 28 June 1914, Archduke Franz Ferdinand of Austria was assassinated by Gavrilo Princip, a Yugoslav nationalist. This one act would begin a chain reaction of events that would lead to war being declared. On 28 July 1914, the first shots were fired, prompting other countries to show support for each other. On 1 August, Germany declared war on Russia and launched an attack on Paris. After neutralizing the threat from France, Germany set her sights on Russia. Britain would not join the war until 5 August 1914 after the German invasion across Europe. The prime minister of Britain, Herbert Henry Asquith, had issued an ultimatum to Germany but with no response from Theobald Bethmann-Hollweg, the German chancellor, Asquith felt there was no other option than to go to war. The assassination of the archduke did not even feature in the local news in Newtownards, and the news of Britain joining the war was not even considered front-page news for the local paper, but did merit a small feature to inform the town.

As soon as Britain had joined the Great War the local men of the Ulster Volunteer Force quickly offered their services to the armed forces when Lord Kitchener asked for 100,000

General Joffre.

KITCHENER'S ULSTER VOLUNTEER ARMY CORPS IN THE MAKING, AT CLANDEBOYE CAMP.

Kitchener's Army.

local men to join the fight. No longer were they a paramilitary organization, prepared to fight against the British and Irish forces for freedom, they had become so much more. Young men had previously been encouraged to join the Ulster Volunteers as an act of responsibility, but now they were told to join the army as well as the Volunteers. Edward Carson offered the services of these men and encouraged them to enlist to fight for Ulster. A division was set up by the Home Office to accommodate the volunteers and they became the 36th (Ulster) Division. As the men enlisted with the armed forces, no one really considered what would happen. Many believed that showing British strength would be enough to win the war. None of the men expected to see action and even fewer predicted the devastation that would fall upon the town in the years to follow.

Local espionage

As the war was beginning to escalate and spread across Europe, a new problem arose. People were warned that there might be spies among them and they could be reporting back to the enemy. This was not as far-fetched as it sounds. Newtownards and North Down had become a ripe recruiting ground for the British army so the enemy may have wanted to observe where most of the troops came from and how they received their basic training.

On 7 August 1914, a German man was arrested on the charge of espionage. Paul George Wentzel lived in the Mine House in an area known locally as Whitespots. This area is where the lead mines

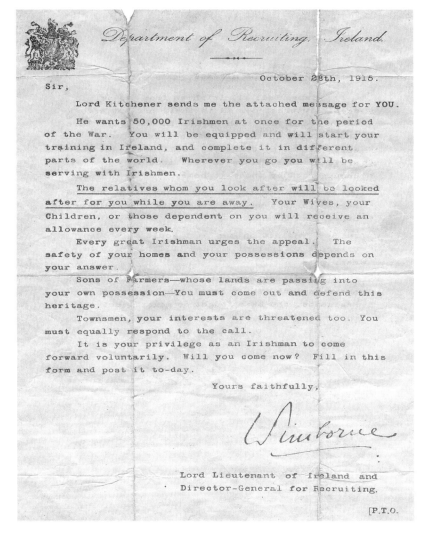

Recruitment letter dated 28 October 1915.

were situated on the outskirts of Newtownards. He was described in the *Newtownards Chronicle* as 'A man of soldierly bearing, apparently 35, cultured, well educated, spoke English fluently.'

His story was an interesting one and prompted suspicion among the people of the town. He had arrived in 1910 in connection with a mining project at Whitespots but the project had closed down after two years. Wentzel had chosen to stay in the area instead of

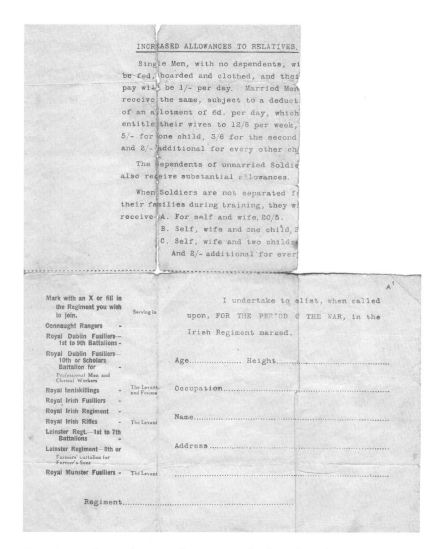

Recruitment letter showing allowances and a form for enlistment.

returning to his native Germany. He did not work and claimed that his brother was financing his stay. Many people had a stereotypical view of Germans and their work ethic. They viewed the German people as hard-working, industrious characters who would not live off another person's money in this way. This image of the hard-working German race fuelled suspicion within the town and rumours of a spy quickly began to circulate. Questions flew around

Joseph Burns, died as the result of gas poisoning.

as to why he was living off his brother's money or why did he *claim* to be living off his brother's money? What if he wasn't doing that? What if it was a lie? What if the mining operation didn't exist? Was it a cover so that the enemy could infiltrate Ireland undetected? With the war just beginning and a sense of paranoia raging through people's minds, Wentzel's house was raided and he was arrested under the Official Secrets Act of 1911. It was believed that he was a German cavalry officer and was communicating information about the British to the enemy. Yet how could this be? He had arrived long before the war had started, but why had he stayed? The locals could not see why he had decided to stay in the area. He lived in a small house, he had not taken a wife nor had any romantic interests in the area. The town had many questions about this strange man that needed to be answered.

The *Newtownards Chronicle* gave a list of the items recovered from Wentzel's house. They included several different drawings which they believed to include those of a semaphore mast, a fort, a furnace, and a rough drawing of a heavy gun and gun embrasure. Several maps were recovered including a large published map of Belfast that showed the harbour, docks and the course of the channel. Other published maps included Aldershot military camp and two railway maps of Great Britain showing the steamboat routes. One item of particular interest was a sheet of paper with the names of four ships' captains written on it; two of the captains were English and the other two were believed to be German. A pocket book that was found contained what were believed to be cypher codes. A page from the Belfast newspaper, the *Northern Whig*, which was dated 5 August 1914, was found and it contained a map of the seat of the war. What interested people about this map were the three routes traced in red pencil, each tracing a different route through Europe. One route was of Berlin through Paris, from Paris to London, and through Holland to London. On the same paper there was blue pencil marking paragraphs referring to the state of feeling between Germany and Great Britain. There were also a number of roughly-made plans of an unidentified area.

The prosecution believed that Wentzel was attempting to obtain information and gather intelligence about the British forces to be passed on to the enemy and all the evidence hung on what was discovered in his house. When questioned in court, Wentzel gave an incredible defence, knocking down every accusation that was thrown at him. He told the jury that the magazines and newspapers did not contain any secrets for winning the war; they were widely-published articles that anyone could buy and read. All the maps were published and available to millions of people around the world. He revealed it was even possible to buy a postcard with a picture of

Scrabo Tower on it in Germany. In fact, copies of the *Chronicle* newspaper were shipped across the world to international readers. He explained that the drawings of the gun embrasure were in fact the foundation of a furnace, and the fort was part of a larger plan for work to be done in the area. As for the pencil lines on the map, one of his local friends had drawn them in an attempt to explain how the mail and postal routes would be affected coming from the British mainland and Europe. When questioned about his military connections, he claimed he had never been in the German forces due to a deformity of one of his hands. This deformity meant that he couldn't hold a rifle properly, something that is required of any soldier and not just in the German forces. He explained that he had attended a military riding school when he was younger but that did not amount to being an officer in the German forces. He was acquitted of all charges of espionage against the British Empire by a jury of his peers. In a shocking twist to this tale, as he was leaving court to return home to Whitespots, he was taken into police custody by military authorities. Despite being a free man after the jury gave its verdict, he was detained in Central Police Station in Belfast as an alien. He was later sent to a British concentration camp on the Isle of Man and was never heard of again. No one knows what became of him after this and any attempts to trace his whereabouts after this have led to a dead end. It seems that although he had been cleared of all charges, the fact that he was

Newtownards Town Hall.

Newtownards High Street.

German with possible military connections was enough for him to be seen as a threat. No one will ever be sure if he was in fact a spy or what happened to him after he left the court that day.

The Rose Show

One of the most important events for the upper classes of Newtownards was the annual Horticultural Show. Rose-breeding was a popular pastime for the Newtownards gardener and the Dixon family had a reputation of being the finest rose-breeders in Ireland. The Newtownards Horticultural Society was forced to cancel its annual show in 1914 due to the war. They believed it would be bad taste to have a flower show when men had already begun to ship out to Europe. They decided that they would save the beauty of the flowers for when the war was over and everyone would be able to enjoy them.

At this stage, people believed that the conflict would not last long and their loved ones would return home after a few weeks. As more men left the town to go to the front in France, the local photography parlours saw a surge in business. Many young soldiers

Heading to war.

decided to have their pictures taken in uniform before setting off. They had not realized that war was a gruesome and bloody business that could kill them. They sat in the parlours, filled with pride in their uniforms. Many believed that the photo for which they were sitting would be a memento of their glory days at war. For most of these men, it was the final picture that would ever be taken of them.

In September 1914, a new division of Lord Kitchener's army was formed. The 36th (Ulster) Division was formed to add thirteen new battalions to three existing army regiments. These included the Royal Irish Fusiliers, the Royal Inniskilling Fusiliers and the Royal Irish Rifles. The 36th (Ulster) Division was heavily recruited from the existing Ulster Volunteer Force. The Volunteers had an advantage over other new recruits as they had experienced military training during their service with the UVF. When it came to basic training, the UVF members excelled in all aspects. For many of these men the war presented an opportunity to show the world what they were capable of.

The massive surge in recruiting in the area meant that there was a need for a military base in the locality. A military centre was set up in the recreation grounds of the town and the Clandeboye Estate in Bangor was used as a training base for new recruits. The existing members of the UVF were trained more in combat and the newest recruits hoped to benefit from the wisdom of the older men who had served in other British wars. After the news that local men had begun dying at the front already, it was important to the higher ranks that the men received the best training in the hope that they would return home.

In a bid to keep the local people informed of what was happening, the local paper ran a section headed 'Who's Who in the Crisis'. Before the war, the people of Newtownards would have had no interest in foreign affairs as there was enough happening in Ulster at the time! However, people wanted to know who they were fighting and why. It's not surprising that the information provided in the local papers was one-sided but some of the information given was also completely inaccurate. While it may have been difficult to explain the complex nature of what had happened and how a series of events had led to the Great War, the simplistic way in which the information was presented to the general public was embarrassing.

A doctor's letter.

As the winter months descended, so did the child-killer, scarlet fever. Scarlet fever was sweeping the area and there were sixty-five reported cases within the town within the last year.

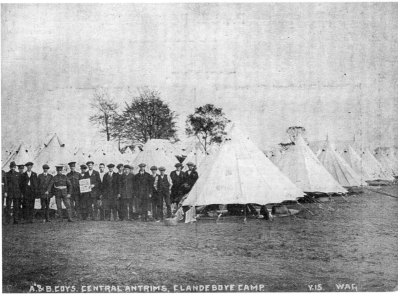

The Antrim UVF training at Clandeboye camp.

The local doctors encouraged mothers to treat the early signs of the fever with broth and cold compresses. At this time there was no cure for scarlet fever, the antibiotics to treat it would not be

Soldiers at Clandeboye camp.

discovered for another fourteen years and scarlet fever was the number one killer of children. This only added to the burden that women were already facing.

13th (S) Battalion, The Royal Irish Rifles, Clandeboye, Co. Down, 1914
One of the first parades in uniform—but no equipment as yet

The 13th Battalion, Royal Irish Rifles at Clandeboye camp in 1914.

Audacious sinking

On 27 October, the people of Ireland were reminded that the threat of war was closer to home than they realized. The battleship HMS *Audacious* was taking part in gunnery exercises when she left Lough Swilly and headed to Loch na Keal in Ireland. Other ships from the 2nd Battalion of the Grand Fleet were also taking part. These included *Ajax*, *Centurion*, *King George V*, *Thunderer*, *Orion* and *Monarch*. In the middle of a turn off Troy Island, the ship detonated an enemy mine that was around 5 metres beneath it at 8.45 am. Captain Cecil Dampier believed that they had been attacked by an enemy submarine and sounded the warning. The other ships of the squadron steamed off to prevent any further attacks from the unseen submarine. At first, the captain thought that he could make the 25-mile trip to the coast and beach the ship. The *Audacious* was still able to make speed at 10 mph but was taking on water rapidly. By 11.00 am the ship was rolling to the port side and the central turbine was submerged.

The crew of the ship was rescued by the light cruiser *Liverpool* and the White Star liner *Olympic*, the elder sister ship of the ill-fated *Titanic*. The *Liverpool* attempted to tow the *Audacious* after the captain had got the bow turned around to sea. All non-essential crew were ordered off the ship and a tow line was secured within thirty minutes. By this time the *Audacious* had begun to sink so badly that she became unmanageable and the tow line snapped. While attempts were made to save the ship, the coastguard in Mulroy, Ireland had sent a message that several ships had been mined within the previous twenty-four hours. On discovering that the threat was from mines and not submarines, the Admiral of the Fleet, Earl Jellicoe, ordered a battleship and a construction officer out to the ship in the hope of repairing her and saving her. As night began to fall, the remaining crew was ordered off the ship. The quarterdeck flooded and the whaler broke loose. As it slid across the deck, more damage was caused and the ship began to sink even faster. By 8.45 pm the decks were underwater and the ship finally capsized. She remained this way until 9.00 pm when explosions began to rip through the ship. Shells that had been safely placed in racks were now able to roam freely before colliding with each other. The explosions threw wreckage 300 metres into the air and struck a petty officer on the *Liverpool* who died of his injuries. The ship finally sank beneath the waves and fell to the sea floor where she remains to this day. She landed upside-down with her rudder detached and her starboard propeller shafts bent.

Although this happened off the coast of Donegal, it was important to the people of Newtownards. As a coastal town with a thriving fishing community, the idea that enemy mines were being placed around the coastline and throughout the Irish Sea without anyone noticing was terrifying. This did not just put the warships in danger but also ordinary men who fished around the coast, and after learning that two other ships had been mined in that area, would the men feel safe enough to fish out there? There was also a sense of paranoia, that if a fishing boat managed to survive the minefield that was out there, what was stopping an enemy submarine from attacking a fishing boat? The German forces would have been aware of the gun-running in April and how different ships were used. Who was to say that the Germans didn't suspect every boat around Belfast and the north coast?

The War Office attempted to keep the sinking a secret and the ship remained on shipping lists for the rest of the war. The British did not want to show any weakness to their enemy by admitting that one of their battleships had been sunk by a mine. However, the problem with trying to keep this secret was the photographs and one moving film that had been taken by the passengers of the *Olympic*. The American passengers were not under British jurisdiction and spoke freely about what they had seen.

Only a short while after the *Audacious* was sunk, HMS *Monmouth* was hit. Able Seaman Samuel Johnston from Donaghadee was killed in action on 1 November 1914 while on board HMS *Monmouth* during the Battle of Coronel, which took place off the coast of Chile. The ship was part of a squadron that was assigned to protect allied shipping vessels. The light cruiser *Glasgow* had picked up on German activities in the area, but the Germans had noticed the *Glasgow* too. The sea was not calm on this day and Force 7 winds caused the waters to foam up and spray. Once the light had faded at around 7.00 pm, the Germans had a massive advantage over the British ships. Not only were the German ships faster but the British ships were lit up against the night sky after a tactical decision made in the hopes of blinding the German gunners with the sun went wrong. Shortly after 7.00 pm the German ships opened fire and the *Monmouth* was engaged in battle with the German battleship *Gneisenau*. The Germans battered the British ships with gunfire and the *Monmouth* took a direct hit at around 7.25 pm. The shell that hit blew the roof off the *Monmouth*'s forward turret and caused a fire. This fire then caused massive explosions as the ammunition caught fire. It was these explosions that blew the entire turret off the ship. At around 8.00 pm the *Monmouth* managed to put out her fires and attempted to turn but had begun listing too much. When the German ship SMS *Nürnberg* discovered the stricken *Monmouth*, she launched a torpedo attack that missed the vessel. When the ship refused to surrender and turned towards the cruiser, the Germans opened fire. At around 10.00 pm, the *Monmouth* capsized completely and took her entire crew of 735 men, including Able Seaman Johnston, with her. The rough seas prevented any rescue attempt being made for the crews of the *Monmouth* or the *Good Hope*. The *Good Hope* had suffered around thirty-five hits when she went down beneath the waves in the darkness. Altogether there were 1,570 lives lost off the coast of Chile in the Pacific Ocean that day.

There was no doubt that any young man of Newtownards was ready to lay down his life for king and country, but for some the rejection of not being accepted into the forces was too much to bear. One young man who was refused entry to the army on medical

The King commands me

to assure you of the true sympathy

of His Majesty and The Queen

in your sorrow.

Kitchener's letter of sympathy.

grounds attempted suicide in his home. James McCauley was deemed unfit for active service because of problems with his kidneys and on 2 December 1914 he cut his own throat with a razor blade in front of his young sister. It was her screams that alerted their father to what had happened and saved his life. James needed fourteen stitches to his neck and claimed he had no memory of the incident. It was declared that it was temporary insanity brought on by being rejected from joining the army that led to James's actions that day.

However, James's actions were not an isolated incident. Young men who had been rejected from service began to act errantly and make a nuisance of themselves in the local bars. Drinking and reckless behaviour began to become an issue among the men who were left behind. Like James McCauley, some had been refused on medical grounds but others refused to join the war effort in any way. Choosing to stay behind was not an issue as if every man enlisted then there would be none left at home; it was the lack of responsibility that angered people. The townsfolk did not expect the community doctor or the farmers to drop everything and join the war. However, there were men who had jobs that could easily be left behind and they refused to join. Being part of the war effort was seen as something to be incredibly proud of and those who didn't want to join were called cowards. Continued slander and mocking drove those men to the bars where they drank themselves silly before getting into a fist fight with whoever mocked them.

As the year came to a close, the women of Comber continued their work for the war relief fund. They had a collection in order to send Christmas gifts to the men at the front. Some money was collected for the 3rd Cavalry Brigade under General Gough, some for the sailors, and other small sums went to the Irish Guards, the Highland regiments and the 44th Battery. Meanwhile the Ladies Comfort Committee worked on sending parcels to each of the Newtownards men serving their country. They asked the locals to donate good pipes, strong leather gloves and knitted items. Although the women had good intentions regarding helping the soldiers, there was some rivalry between them as to who had the most family members serving in the armed forces and the competitiveness of 'who was helping more' began extending into the relief fund. Although it could be considered a good thing that the women were competing to give the most help, it sometimes resulted in fights between them!

Shortly after the Christmas period, letters home would be full of stories of an unofficial truce between the opposing sides over Christmas. Captain Mervyn Stronge Richardson was one officer who made contact with the Germans on the other side of the trenches and agreed on the truce for the day. The Germans had suggested the ceasefire first and had sent a chocolate cake to the British as a gift. The British accepted the gift and returned the favour with some tobacco. The guns went quiet and carols were sung on the Western Front as the forces joined together for a brief period to exchange small gifts, collect the dead and have a game of football. Many of the Germans spoke English and both sides agreed that they were fed up with the fighting and just wanted to go home. The officers, both German and British, were less than

Mill Street, Comber   Co. Down

Barefoot children in Mill Street, Comber look on as people go about their day.

happy with this talk. Spirits were high before the men returned to the fighting and bloodshed a few days later. For those at home, it must have been a relief that the soldiers did not have to fight over the Christmas period. This brief ceasefire showed that peace was possible between the two sides. It also caused a lot of people to question why the war was still continuing. People believed that if the men at the front who had to do the killing could put down their weapons so easily, then those in command could surely begin negotiating a truce to end the war.

CHAPTER TWO

1915: Deepening the Conflict

The New Year dawned and life in the town attempted to go on as normal. The town inspectors began their year by carrying out their annual inspections of the local shops. The belief was that life should appear to be continuing as normal and it was important to ensure that everything was as it should be. Wartime economics started to play a part in daily life as people had to begin rationing their food and clothes. After the slight indulgence of the holiday season, many people had to cut back on little luxuries. Most people looked forward to this year and hoped that their loved ones would be coming home soon, but the news continued to travel home that men were still dying. The first casualty of the year was Sapper Nathaniel Ferguson who died on 1 January. Sapper Ferguson was born in Comber, just outside of Newtownards, and he died of blood poisoning in France.

At the beginning of 1915, the locals got to see Sir Edward Carson make his way to Bangor to inspect the 1st Battalion of the North Down Regiment UVF. Although many members of the UVF had chosen to join the 36th (Ulster) Division, many others had decided that Ireland still needed to be defended. Rumours had been circulating that the Irish Nationalists were still attempting to bring guns into the country but nothing had been confirmed. Unlike the men who didn't enlist in the war effort, these men were treated differently and with respect. As the war raged on across Europe, the conflicts back home had shifted focus. No longer were people so concerned with Home Rule, but the thought of it lingered on. All eyes were on the war and news of loved ones dying continued to pour in. As more men died, more left the town to fight and the people began to feel the strain of having so many good men leave. Civil disputes began to surface between neighbours

Mill Street in Comber with the railway arch in the distance.

and women argued over who had given up more men to the fight. Depression filled the hearts of many citizens. Some carried on as normal while others drowned their sorrows in the local bars. Alcohol-fuelled fights became a common reason for arrests, while warring neighbours filled the courthouse.

A hero called Paddy is born

The Mayne family were prominent businessmen and landowners in Newtownards. During the Great War the family was blessed with a son, Robert Blair 'Paddy' Mayne who was born on 11 January 1915. Paddy was the sixth of seven children to be born at Mount Pleasant. This family home is rumoured to be one of the places that stored weapons from the UVF gun-running operation from the year before. Robert was named after his second cousin who was a serving soldier in the Great War and his name would be

Two men pose on the road outside the spinning mill in Comber.

his legacy. Little did the family know that Robert would go on to be one of the founding members of the Special Air Service (SAS) during the Second World War, a solicitor and an Ireland rugby union international.

Death of the Marquis of Londonderry

On 8 February, the town received the devastating news that the Marquis of Londonderry had died. Charles Vane-Tempest-Stewart was the 6th Marquis of Londonderry. His death was a devastating blow to the town as he was an avid supporter of the Ulster Volunteer Force and opposed Home Rule. He died of pneumonia at the age of 62. When the news broke, there was an outpouring of grief from the locals. Many people had the pleasure of knowing him personally. Others had met him briefly or knew of his work in Irish politics. The marquis was well-known and loved in the town and his sudden passing was a shock to the community. His wife announced that she would be taking over his official duties and would continue to support the Unionist movement in Ulster.

Murder most foul

William 'Willie' Quinn was a 23-year-old man who was well-known and liked in the town. However, on 14 February the town was shaken by the news that he had been murdered outside his home at Flush Hall. He had lived with his stepfather Samuel Heron, Samuel's wife and Samuel's son. Flush Hall was located on the Scrabo Road at the base of Scrabo Hill, not far from the Mayne family home of Mount Pleasant on the Belfast Road. Three years after the death of William's father, William's mother had married Samuel Heron. After her death, Samuel had become William's guardian and he had remarried again. The family tree had become slightly complicated because of the deaths and marriages over the years.

Shortly after midnight, Mrs Heron, Samuel's new wife who he had married a few years after the death of William's mother,

Flush Hall was the site of William 'Willie' Quinn's murder in 1915.

heard something outside the home. She was woken from her sleep and when she went to investigate, Mr Heron came in through the front door. She believed the noise was dogs fighting outside and after her husband had assured her it was nothing, she returned to bed. A few hours later she would be woken again, this time by the doorbell ringing, and this time it would be William she would meet at the door. Badly beaten and bloody, William had crawled from the garden to the front door and rung the bell before collapsing on the porch. He had been walking home after meeting some friends in a public house in the town when he was attacked just outside his home. When he walked through the gates at Flush Hall, he was attacked and brutally beaten by someone who was hidden in the darkness. When he was found by Mrs Heron, she saw immediately that Willie had been badly beaten. He was covered in blood and also dirt from the garden.

Mrs Heron summoned the doctor and the police to the house immediately. When the doctor arrived, William claimed that he

Flush Hall, the site of Willie Quinn's murder in 1915.

wasn't drunk and he hadn't seen his attacker. At first he believed he was the victim of a robbery as his silver pocket watch was missing, but the watch was later found in the garden where he had been attacked. With no other items of his missing, it became clear that he had been beaten for a far more sinister reason, but who would want to hurt such a lovely young man? With no suspects or witnesses the police had very little to go on. Even William didn't know who had hurt him or why.

Although the police had very little to go on, they launched an investigation in the hope that something would turn up or that Willie would remember something. It was rumoured that the attacker had hidden behind one of the gate pillars at the front of the property and waited for him to return home. The attacker had hit him repeatedly around the head with a blunt object or had kicked him repeatedly in the head while he lay helpless on the ground. This left him with several large cuts and bruises over his face and neck. Although he had initially survived the attack, he eventually died from his injuries on the following Monday. The public demanded that the person responsible for this horrible crime be brought to justice quickly. To the people of Newtownards, their town was not a place where people were attacked in their own garden and murder would not be tolerated.

If it was not enough that a young man was brutally beaten to death in his own garden, a cruel twist of fate would see young Willie being buried on the day that he was supposed to marry his sweetheart Miss Minnie Laverty. On 18 February 1915, as the funeral cortège set off to lay William at his final resting-place, a shocking turn of events would occur. William's stepfather, Samuel Heron, was arrested as the coffin was being carried out of the town. Shock and dismay filled the crowd as Samuel Heron was led away for questioning by the local police. During the investigation of the attack Samuel Heron could not account for his whereabouts on that fateful night and this made him a suspect, but why would he want to kill his stepson?

On the death of William's mother, Samuel had become William's guardian and trustee of his late wife's estate. Samuel and William did not just live together as father and son, they also worked together at the Ulster Print Works Limited where Samuel was the manager. Samuel was described by those who knew him as a peaceful and law-abiding citizen who would lend a hand to anyone that needed it. However, all was not as it seemed. Samuel Heron had access to William's accounts and had spent all of his inheritance, including the annual income from the rented houses owned by the late Mr Quinn, William's father. Samuel justified his actions by claiming that the money was used to help raise him and pay his keep at Flush Hall. The only money William had ever received was his wages from the print works. William had reportedly spoken with his stepfather not long before the attack about receiving his inheritance as he was to be married on 18 February 1915 and was setting up a new home in the town for himself and his new bride.

The time came and passed for Samuel to give William his money, yet William did not see any of his inheritance. Part of the money he should have been receiving was the rent from seven houses in Newry that were owned by his late father. As the police investigation continued, it became clear that Samuel Heron was in a great deal of debt. During the court proceedings people began coming forward to testify that Samuel Heron owed them money. Money was owed to the bank, to the family grocer, to the local hardware store and to a draper, and these were only some of the debts that came to light. Other people testified that Samuel had tried to destroy evidence of his crime and had tried to enlist their help. A wooden mallet was found with traces of blood in the groove of the head. It was this item that the police believed was used to beat William as he walked in through the garden gate. Once the attacker had beaten William to the ground, he had begun kicking him in the head. William's head was the only site of his injuries and the court decided that it had been a premeditated attack in the hope of ending William's life. The most damning evidence came from a young worker who claimed that Samuel had asked him to help clean the mallet and destroy any evidence that he was involved in the attack.

The town was left suffering from the shock of a young man being murdered outside his own home, and nobody could believe that Samuel Heron had killed his stepson over money. The murder would go down in local history as a brutal attack on an innocent man from an uncaring stepfather.

Women in the war

All across Britain women were campaigning for equal rights and the suffragists tirelessly fought for equality for women. Women wanted freedom, the right to vote, equal pay and the right to work in any job they wanted. While many women staged protests, the women of Ulster formed the Ulster Women's Unionist Council and they were fighting in their own way. Although women were concerned about voting and their rights, they also had other things to worry about that didn't affect their counterparts in England. With the possibility of a civil war in Ireland and the outbreak of the Great War, the council formed a new nursing corps. The Ulster Volunteer Nursing Corps was part of the Ulster Volunteer Force and was designed to deal with any casualties that occurred during times of conflict. Normally nurses received three years of training but these ladies only had to take a short course that would provide them with basic first-aid training. A great rivalry began between the two nursing factions, and the Ulster Volunteer Force nurses were considered stupid and untrained by their professionally-trained counterparts. The Clandeboye training camp served as a training base for the local soldiers destined for the battlefield and as a training centre for the Ulster Volunteer Force Nursing Corps.

Despite the image of female oppression in the early twentieth century, the women of Newtownards were very capable. Most of the women in the town worked, ran a home and raised their families with great efficiency. An Ulster woman in the early twentieth century needed to do everything done by a modern woman today, but without the time- and labour-saving mod cons of the present day. Despite being ahead of the times on the work and domestic fronts, it was their lack of other rights that made them support the suffragists' cause. Many women from Newtownards were working women who desired the same rights as a man. Women worked in the mills, in the fields and anywhere else that they could. As well as working full-time, these women still managed to run their homes with precision and raise their families. For some households in Newtownards, the woman was the head of the house in the absence of a husband or other man. Some of these women had been abandoned by their husbands or their men had died. Without a man in the house, there were certain legal actions that

UVF nurses.

a woman couldn't undertake, such as voting. By the time the war had started, there were more than 1,000 Ulster women involved with the suffragette movement. These ladies took part in rallies outside mills in Belfast to help give the working woman a voice. Between 1912 and 1914, thirty-five women from Ulster had been arrested and given prison sentences for their part in militant acts in a bid to secure the female right to vote. When war was declared against the Central forces, all members of the suffragette movement had been released from prison. The women took this opportunity to help with the war effort at home as the men were shipped out to fight. The women showed incredible dedication to supporting the troops with fund-raising, welfare parcels and supporting members of the community who had lost a loved one in the conflict. The women did not know it at the time but the support networks that they formed at this point would be a necessity for many years after the war.

North Down Cricket Club Pavilion, Comber 1061

North Down Cricket Club pavilion, Comber.

As well as the nursing corps, several comfort committees were set up. The small population of the area meant that there was a great community spirit when it came to people supporting each other. The Newtownards Comforts Committee began working to ensure that 'their boys at the front' had items that would make life a little better while away from their families. Some of the most important things were knitted items such as socks and jumpers, and cigarettes, tobacco or pipes. The committees would be responsible for drumming up as much support as they could for the soldiers and hoped to play a part on the front line, even if that came in the form of socks and wooden pipes.

The beginning of Neuve Chapelle

On 10 March 1915, the first day of the Battle of Neuve Chapelle took place in France, in which allied forces hoped to break through the German lines to recapture the town. The French forces were exhausted after trying to hold the line and the hope lay in the new British offensive. The Royal Flying Corps (RFC) took some photos

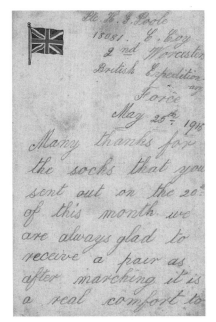

Thank-you card from the soldiers for socks that had been sent out to the front lines.

over the land that needed to be conquered and bombed the railway lines in poor weather conditions. Rifleman James Carnduff was killed on the first day of the offensive while serving with the 1st Battalion, Royal Irish Rifles. As the battle entered Day 2, another Newtownards man perished. Rifleman Alexander Gibson was also serving with the 1st Battalion, Royal Irish Rifles and he was just 19 years old. Day 3 was reported to have been the bloodiest of days when fifty men of the 1st Battalion, Royal Irish Rifles perished on the battlefield. After the bloodshed of Day 3, the soldiers were ordered to prepare for a new attack. However, the information gathered by the allied forces did not give the correct number of German soldiers holding the line and this miscalculation cost the lives of hundreds of men from across the British army. The allies were able to take control of an area, but were too disorganized afterwards. They couldn't get communications up and running quickly enough and too much ammunition was used to gain ground.

HMS *Bayano*

As mentioned earlier in the Introduction, on a clear day the coastline of Scotland is easily seen from the shores of Strangford Lough. On 11 March 1915, at 5.15 am, HMS *Bayano* was torpedoed off the coast of Scotland and sank before the life-rafts could be manned with nearly 200 lives lost. Only twenty-six men were pulled from the water and many men died because they were asleep at the time of the attack. The strong current of the Irish Sea took the bodies around the coastlines of Ireland and Scotland. On the coast of the Ards peninsula, seven bodies of those who had died washed up upon the shore. The local community ensured that the bodies were buried in local graveyards with the care and consideration that they deserved. Among them were Able Seaman Frederick William Chater, Leading Seaman Edgar J. Spracklin, Private A.G. Bain and Able Seaman W.A. Wellstead. Two sailors and one Royal Marine could not be identified. Most of the bodies washed up on the Isle of Man and the locals there treated the dead with the same respect as the locals of Newtownards had given their fellow sailors.

From the beginning of April it was decided that public house opening hours should be restricted in order to curtail the amount of drunken behaviour occurring in the town. Such behaviour had become a serious problem for the police and law enforcement in the area since the New Year. Men were going insane with alcohol in their systems and had started fighting with each other. At the more extreme end of the scale, some were attempting suicide due to the shame of not being able to serve with Kitchener's Army.

Mill View in Comber had a mixture of old and new houses.

On the other side of the Atlantic, America was under prohibition laws, preventing people from drinking alcohol at all. To consider enforcing a complete ban on alcohol in Newtownards was laughable. Even the attempts to prevent men drinking themselves stupid would be difficult enough to enforce by law. It was hoped that the community would use social pressure to prevent any more drunken behaviour.

RMS *Lusitania* and HMS *Goliath*

On 7 May 1915, one of the biggest tragedies in maritime history occurred. In the previous week the German embassy had released a statement about the British ocean liner RMS *Lusitania* and how she was a potential target for German U-boats. The press released a statement warning people about possible attacks, but most did not take the threat seriously as only a few decided to cancel their tickets. The luxury liner was often compared to the *Olympic*-class ships that had been built in Belfast by Harland and Wolff. The ship left port on schedule on 1 May 1915, heading from New York to Britain. A U-boat torpedoed the *Lusitania* when she was 11 miles off the coast of Ireland. The torpedo struck the vessel, causing an explosion, but it was the second unexplained internal explosion that sent the ship to the bottom of the ocean in less than twenty minutes. Only 761 of the 1,962 people on board survived the attack. It was rumoured that some of the passengers were from Newtownards but it was the deaths of 128 out of 139 American citizens on board that caused outrage among the American public. This attack would see President Woodrow Wilson reconsider America's neutral stance on the war. The Germans justified the attack by claiming that the *Lusitania* was carrying large amounts of ammunition, making her a legitimate target. The British government claimed that there was no ammunition on board and the Germans had breached the Cruiser Rules by attacking a civilian vessel. However, before the war the ship had been fitted with compartments to carry ammunition across the Atlantic. It wasn't until the 1980s that a warning was issued to divers who wanted to salvage the wreck.

36th (Ulster) Division parading down Chichester Street, Belfast

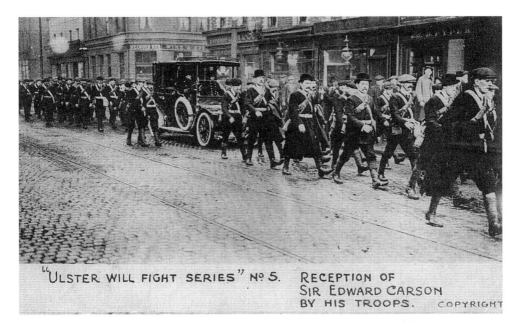

"ULSTER WILL FIGHT SERIES" Nº 5.   RECEPTION OF SIR EDWARD CARSON BY HIS TROOPS.   COPYRIGHT

U.V.F.—SOUTH BELFAST REGIMENT EN ROUTE FOR BALMORAL, 27TH SEPT., 1913.

Publishers—Hurst & Co., Fine Art Warehouse, Belfast.

(A) Reception of Edward Carson by his troops. (B) The UVF: South Belfast Regiment en route to Balmoral, 27 September 1913.

The date of 13 May saw the destruction of the ship HMS *Goliath*. As the vessel was anchored off Cape Helles in Morto Bay, she was torpedoed by a Turkish destroyer. Stoker 1st Class William Ernest Beringer, Boy 1st Class Alfred Henry Victor Gadd and Stoker 1st Class Hector Hiles were three Newtownards men on board who died when the ship was lost. Some 570 men were lost out of a crew of 750.

Unionist politics

In May 1915, Unionist politics would take an interesting turn as Edward Carson was appointed attorney general. He was appointed after the coalition government was formed following the Shell Crisis (the shortage of artillery shells on the front lines) of 1915. At the end of 1914, it had become clear that ammunition supply was becoming a problem. The heavy use of shells to break enemy lines was criticized by many national newspapers. The Battle of Neuve Chapelle is just one example of how much ammunition was used by soldiers to gain ground. More than 30 per cent of available ammunition was used at the front on the first day alone. The government realized at this point in the war that the only way for the British troops to survive at the front was to instigate rationing at home. In the preceding months Newtownards had been undergoing rationing to a certain degree, but now it would have to be taken to a whole new level as the government encouraged people to be more frugal and careful about their wastage.

As the summer months came around, new efforts were made to help both the fighting men and the local population. On 5 June, Newtownards held a cake sale in honour of the soldiers. The Saturday market was a well-known trading event for shoppers in the centre of the town. This Saturday in particular it hosted the event in the hope of raising funds. The sale was well-advertised and people came from all over to help support the troops. Unlike every other year, the celebrations of 12 July passed without any mention in the local papers. Many of the members of the Orange Lodges were in Europe. The parades and marches of previous years were small and went unnoticed.

On 24 July, the *Newtownards Chronicle* published a letter from a soldier who called himself 'The last Newtownards man in India'. Gunner T. McCreadie was a friend of another local man, Samuel

Photos from the Clandeboye camp.

Walker, and the two of them were career soldiers together. Driver Walker had been serving with the 7th Battery, Royal Field Artillery when he was killed in action on 4 April but there had been no mention of his passing in the local paper. Gunner McCreadie was a regular reader of the paper and having noticed that there had been no notification of his friend's death, he penned a letter asking for a small space so that he could inform others of it. The letter said:

> Would you kindly allow me a small place in your weekly paper to convey my deepest sympathy to the relatives of the late Driver S. Walker, who died on 5 April, 1915 [*sic*]. We were great chums since I knew him about ten years ago; and being the last Newtownards man in India, I was very sorry indeed when I received the sad news. I was waiting an answer to a letter which I sent him, but I am sorry to say it reached there too late, and this grieved me more than I can say. The letter I received from his Sergeant Major did not say where he had died, and being a regular reader of your paper I did not see his name mentioned. I trust this will come to the notice of all who knew him in Newtownards. I shall be greatly indebted to you if you will grant me this small favour.

Letters like this had become more common as more men died and other soldiers wanted to pay their respects.

Another letter came to town and described a different young man who had also died. Like many young men in the area, George Jamison was learning a trade before the outbreak of the war. Before he joined the 1st Battalion, Royal Irish Rifles, George was an apprentice weaver. When he was killed in action on 29 July he was known as 'The soldier who died with a smile on his face', as the rector of the Church of Ireland had acknowledged the comments made in a letter to the Jamison family from a fellow soldier, Corporal D. Wilkinson. In the letter he said:

> We all miss him badly here, he was such a good fellow, always in the best of spirits. I might tell you that he died with a smile. He and I were just after passing a joke. He was showing me the rose and the handkerchief you had sent him, then he sat down to write a letter. I don't think he got it finished. He got up again to have a shot at them, as he said, when he was hit. He got it right through the

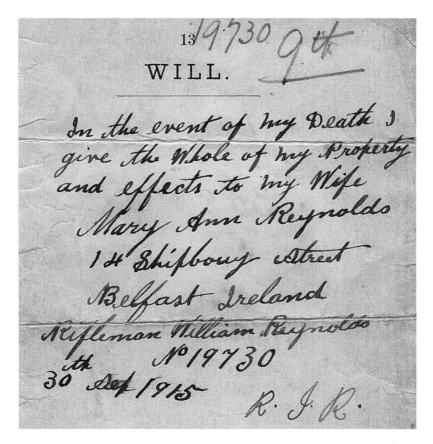

A soldier's will. Rifleman William Reynolds wished to leave the whole of his property and effects to his wife.

head. He did not suffer any pain for he was laughing when he was hit, and that is how he fell, smiling.

Scandal at the 'big house'

Although this was a time of progressive women in Ireland, there was still a social stigma attached to unwed mothers. It was particularly shameful if the child was born as a result of an affair. On 31 July, there would be a tragic discovery made in one of the 'big houses'. A domestic servant would kill her newborn baby in one of the most gruesome ways possible: she cooked it. The young girl, who was not named in the local papers to protect her identity, had just given birth. Nobody knew for sure who the father of the child was. There were rumours that it was her employer's baby but as no one knew who she was, they had no clue about the employer's identity. The baby was discovered when someone in the house smelled burning coming from the oven. When they investigated the source of the smell, they were horrified to discover the burned body of a newborn baby in the bottom of the oven. The judge overseeing the case ruled that the girl was suffering from insanity. The judge could not believe that a sane woman could possibly hurt a child in this way. Rumours circulated for months afterwards as to who it was and who the father might be.

Rose Day and the War Relief Fund

Despite everything that was happening around them, the people of Newtownards were determined to help with the war effort. On 7 August 1915, more than 180 women and girls took to the streets of the town for Rose Day. The local flower nursery had donated their prize-winning Dixon roses to be sold in order to raise money for the war fund. Even children as young as 5 years old were doing their best for the troops. Young Kitty McAlea collected money for cigarettes to send to the troops. The Red Cross regularly had appeals in the town to help raise money and held workshops to teach first aid in Londonderry School. The Women's Committee and the British Red Cross worked closely together at this time in order to help as many people as possible.

One of the main reasons why the first-aid courses were so important was to help the wounded troops. As part of the recovery process, soldiers were shipped back to Britain and cared for in local communities. Wounded soldiers were provided for and entertained by the women of Newtownards. The women would often travel to the Ulster Volunteer Force hospital in Belfast or to Holywood Military Convalescent Hospital in Belfast. Every time the women visited the soldiers, they took small care packages, they sang songs and provided entertainments.

The Red Cross helped the Women's Committee to make appeals to help the war effort. Most appeals were for cigarettes and warm clothes that could be sent to the soldiers in the trenches. Family finances were growing tighter for most people but they tried to donate what they could to help.

For the Boy Scouts, 28 August was a momentous day as Lord Baden-Powell came to inspect his troops at Cliftonville Football Club in Belfast. The boys from the Newtownards scouts travelled to Belfast for the day in order to parade in front of their commanding officer. The Newtownards troop was one of many that paraded in the football ground on that day. The Boy Scouts were seen as the third line of defence against the enemy during times of war. Although they did not receive military training, they were trained in vital survival skills that could help in saving a local community.

Orlock Hill shooting

After the arrest and highly-publicized trial of Paul George Wentzel, the German spy, in Newtownards the previous year, everyone was on guard about the possibility of finding more spies in the area. Hysteria had gripped the north of Ireland and everyone who had any connection with Germany was treated with caution and as a possible threat to national security. Reports began to surface of German nationals being questioned by the police and harassed by locals. It did not matter if there was any substance to the accusations; if you were German, you were a suspect. The paranoia even extended to people who associated with Germans. Even the landlords who allowed Germans to rent a property or a room were considered to be traitors by the locals.

This paranoia led to the belief that certain areas could be at risk. Orlock Hill was a place that could be of tactical value to the enemy, an idea that may never have been thought of until the trial the year before. Guards had been placed in certain areas, including Orlock. On 18 September, a guard was performing his rounds when he spotted somebody riding a bicycle. The guard called out to the unknown person and told them to identify themselves. The unknown cyclist was challenged by the guard a number of times and when he didn't respond to the guard's orders to turn around, the guard opened fire. The cyclist was shot and wounded as he fell from his bicycle. However, when the guard caught up to the man, he realized that he was a local person who happened to be deaf.

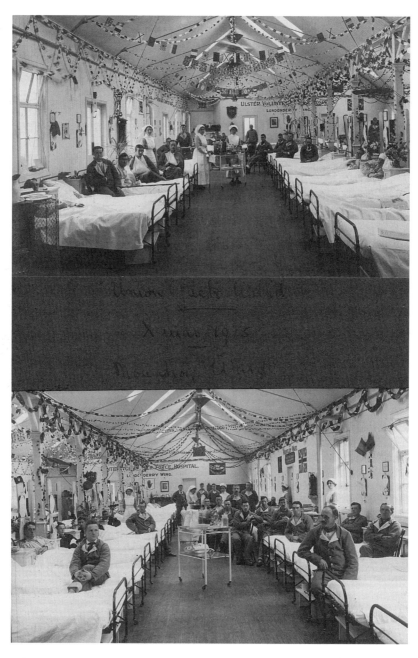

Christmas 1915 at the UVF hospital.

Captain O'Lone

Captain Walter Percy O'Lone had moved to Loughriscouse, a townland between Newtownards and Donaghadee, from Belfast with his mother and father. His father was Quartermaster Sergeant John O'Lone of the Victoria Barracks in Belfast who had become a local hero when he had re-enlisted at the age of 73. Walter was one of eleven children and was the first of the sons to die during the war. He was killed in action while serving with the 2nd Battalion, Royal Irish Rifles on 25 September 1915, at the age of 25. He had been awarded the Distinguished Conduct Medal after showing great bravery by running important messages while under heavy shelling and gunfire.

The UVF hospital, 1915.

The last Newtownards man to die in this year of the war would perish on 24 December but not in the trenches. Sergeant George Hamilton died in Wellington Barracks in Dublin on Christmas Eve (his cause of death is not known). This was when hundreds of soldiers on both sides of the trenches took part in an unofficial truce over the festive period, this despite warnings from officers that there would be consequences for fraternizing with the enemy. After the previous year, when soldiers had laid down their guns for two days, commanding officers were left in shock. A repeat of the truce this year was unacceptable and those in charge were not prepared to have their men regarded as soft. Orders were given to the front: kill the enemy, even at Christmas.

While the men struggled and broke their orders in the trenches, Christmas continued much as normal for the people of

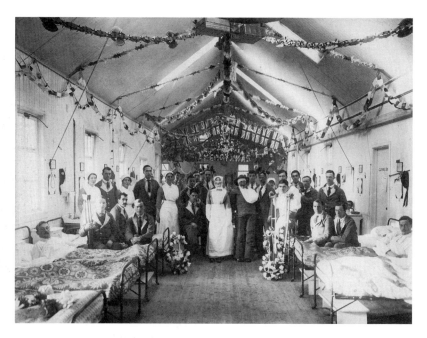

The UVF hospital at Christmas.

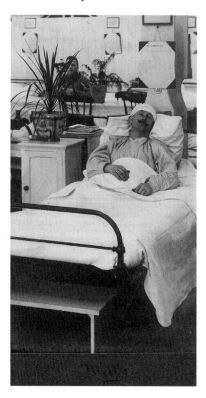

The UVF hospital, 1915.

Newtownards. While many mourned the loss of loved ones, others felt grateful that their loved ones were still alive, even though they were serving somewhere in Europe.

With the Great War now having been raging for more than a year, the Home Rule crisis had been pushed to the back of everybody's minds. People believed that the sacrifice that was being made would shed a good light on the people of Ulster. Surely a country that had given so many of her sons would not be cast out to be ruled by an Irish Republic? However, the people who wanted Home Rule had the same idea; they had sent many of their own out to the front in order to win the favour of the Crown and have the Home Rule Bill passed. Only time would tell how the British Parliament was planning on 'rewarding' Ireland after the war.

Robert Lightbody of Newtownards, killed at Gallipoli

CHAPTER THREE

1916: The Realization

As this new year dawned, people realized how bad the war really was. Families were torn apart as young women were widowed and older women were made childless as their brave serving sons died in action. The local clothes-makers began experiencing a huge demand for mourning clothes as a direct result of the war. Some establishments claimed they could barely keep up with the demand as more and more men perished at the front. It was said, in local rumours, that many of the women who lost their husbands and their sons died of heartbreak at such losses. On a certain level, it was true: many of the women who were left widowed and childless died suddenly and many people believed it was the loss of their loved ones that had broken their hearts. Their possessions and homes ultimately went to auction as no living relative could be found to claim them.

Seeing the loss of life around them – from both the widows left with no family and the men dying at the front – many people decided to search for long-lost family around the world in the hope of making a connection with some long-forgotten branch of their family tree. People began placing adverts in the papers in search of forgotten relatives. The heartbreak of the widows was not confined to the older generations; many young women died and left young children behind with no one to care for them. There was a huge outcry for foster parents to provide loving homes for the orphaned children in the area. Many of these children had turned to stealing in order to survive and were becoming a nuisance for the police and the courts.

For the women who did survive the heartbreak, a different battle raged on. Many of the mothers who were widowed found themselves battling with their children. With their fathers dead, some children began skipping school and getting themselves into trouble with the law. These mothers had to face a court appearance because of their unruly children. For the most part, the judges were understanding of the situation and issued attendance orders. The hope was that these orders would make the children attend school and stay out of mischief. However, some mothers were not so fortunate and a short prison term for the mother was seen as the only option.

For the men who were left behind at home it was a dark time. Those who chose not to go to war were viewed as cowards. Those who couldn't go due to being deemed unfit for service began to suffer from depression. They were left behind and kept hearing of their friends or relatives dying on the battlefield. The town's public houses were full of these men who chose to drown their sorrows instead of helping in other ways. At this time prohibition was still in force in America and the people of Newtownards were asked to follow in the Americans' footsteps. Although drinking was still legal, it was frowned upon. Comber Whiskey was a local favourite drink in the pubs. Drinking was not only seen as a waste of money, it caused trouble too. Drunken behaviour became a common occurrence in the courts with heavy fines being imposed. One Newtownards man even ended up dead at the very beginning of the year. After drinking too much alcohol in one of the public houses, he took his own life and he would not be the only one to do this. For some men their despair and judgement from others became too much and they decided that taking their own lives was the only answer available to them. These men were considered to be suffering from temporary insanity brought on by depression. The depression was caused by not being allowed to help with the war effort as a serving soldier. These men were caught in a vicious circle. If they had been allowed to enlist, they would have been a hindrance on the front line because of their health problems. However, with their enlistment refused, they became a problem in the town as they drowned their sorrows in whiskey and beer.

Drunken behaviour was not the only thing on which the courts came down hard as people who didn't pay their road tax were also dealt with. It may have seemed like a small and petty thing to enforce while a global conflict was raging, but those in charge

Comber Whiskey.

Spinning Mill in Comber with the Enler River running alongside.

had decided that life in Newtownards would continue as normal so taxes had to be paid and children had to be in school.

As the war continued, people were becoming more aware of the 'Aliens' in Belfast who were travelling to the outlying towns. By the end of January, paranoia had continued to grow among the people of Ireland, and when faced with a foreign person they were unsure if they could be trusted. More and more people, who were originally from different countries, continued to be questioned and not only by the law enforcers; the people who lived around them also viewed them with suspicion. The fear of having spies in the community became so great that anyone, no matter how long they had lived in the area, could be treated with suspicion and fear. The community was on an emotional knife edge with the continual stream of death notices that seemed to come on a daily basis. Thoughts of having people who might be responsible for their loved ones' deaths living among them were enough to fuel the fires of racism.

One of the few men who had the honour of being buried at home was David Stratton. A keen footballer and a member of the Ards Air Gun Club, he was a well-loved man within the town. As well as his job in the Glen Printing and Finishing Works Ltd, he was also the scoutmaster of the 2nd Newtownards Troop of Boy Scouts. When the war began he enlisted with the Ulster Division Engineers. During his time at the front he was promoted to company quartermaster sergeant, before being taken ill with pneumonia. He recovered from his illness but it returned, leaving him hospitalized in England. His wife was sent for and she was with him when he died on 27 February. Being so close to home, his body was shipped across the Irish Sea so that he could be buried in Movilla graveyard.

The Fisher family would finally get the closure they needed surrounding the disappearance of James Fisher. James, or Jim as he was known, was serving with the 1st Battalion, Royal Irish Rifles in France but had stopped writing home to his family in March 1915. The family was surrounded by hearsay and rumours as to what had happened to him. After his letters stopped coming, he was presumed missing in action. Other soldiers who were writing home began asking their families to pass the sad news of his death on to Jim's wife. They wrote that he had been killed during the

UVF nurses.

Battle of Neuve Chapelle after being shot in the stomach. As the trenches were under heavy enemy fire they were unable to rescue him from the field. It would be a full year before his wife received the official news that he had been killed in March 1915.

For the children, life was not much better. It seemed that bad luck had begun to follow the children of the fallen soldiers. Young Maud Moore had lost her father, William Moore, the year before at Dardanelles, and now at 6 years old she suffered from another terrible twist of fate. While her mother was cooking a meal, Maud's clothes caught fire and she suffered from terrible burns over her body. She survived her injuries but was left permanently scarred.

As the year continued, the shortages of the war began to take hold. A paper shortage meant that all the local newspapers had to be thinned down. The *Newtownards Chronicle* announced in the spring that they would be making the paper much smaller and thinner.

After the previous year's problems with foreign aliens, law enforcement began cracking down on people for being lax in their civic duty of reporting such people in the area. One such woman

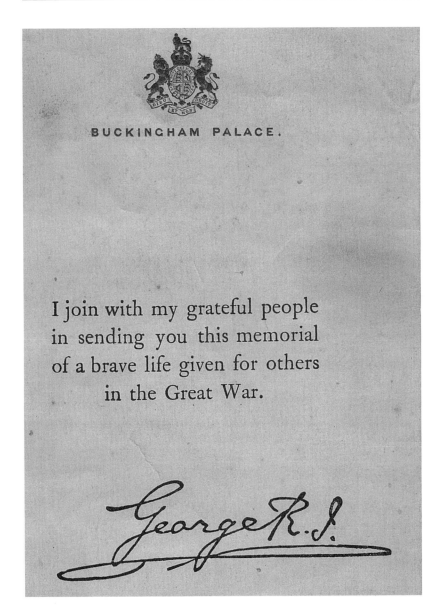

Memorial letter.

was Eliza Jane Norris, a lodging-keeper on Movilla Street. She was summoned to court for the offence of failing to keep a proper register of those over the age of 14 staying in her lodge. Two Italian men, Pasquale Rea and Francis Nocker, were staying with her at her lodging house at this time. They had reported her to the police as they knew she had not properly registered their stay with her. Being an older woman, everyone believed that she simply didn't understand the importance of keeping the register. The court failed to see it that way and took the opportunity to make an example of Ms Norris, showing that this behaviour would not be tolerated in Newtownards. Everyone was expected to play their part in the war effort. Newtownards and the surrounding areas of Bangor, Donaghadee and Holywood were prohibited areas in Ireland under the Alien Restriction (Consolidation) Order. Even people who had lived in the country for years were under suspicion of spying on the local population. A Russian gentleman, Samuel Bonovitz, who had lived in the country for seventeen years, was charged in Belfast Police Court with failing to register himself as an alien. He was outraged by the verdict as he considered himself a citizen of Ireland.

Tragic childhood death

The women of Newtownards worried about their husbands out on the front line but one woman suffered more than some. Ellen Johnston had slowly gone blind over the course of her life and by the birth of her third child her sight had completely deteriorated. Her husband, who served with the Royal Irish Regiment, had been injured at the front at Neuve Chapelle in France. After recovering at home, he returned to the front and was at Dardanelles when tragedy struck. One Monday morning, young Isabella Johnston's clothes caught fire. Her mother had left her alone in the house for a few minutes to speak with a neighbour. Ellen was getting the baby checked over by a neighbour after she had heard a bump and thought that the baby had fallen. Being concerned that the infant was injured, Ellen went to her next-door neighbour for help. During the short time that 3-year-old Isabella was left unattended, her clothes caught fire. Not knowing what to do, the young child screamed as she ran out of the house into the arms of the very neighbour who was checking over her younger sibling. Although the fire was quickly extinguished, the shock of what happened was too much for the 3-year-old to bear. Isabella Johnston died of severe shock the following evening after suffering burns to the left side of her body.

Renewable energy

It was mentioned in the Introduction that one of the many beautiful areas in Newtownards is Strangford Lough. Famous for its fishing and strong currents, the lough is not just beautiful but considered a dangerous place as the powerful undertow could easily drown even an experienced swimmer. Today the lough has turbines that provide power to the local area but the idea originally came about in 1916. It was planned that the estuary of the lough would be fitted with turbines so that the powerful currents would generate electricity. It was believed that the strength of the current on any given day could generate 19,000 or 20,000 horse power within two-and-a-half hours. Batteries would store any extra energy to provide power all year round to homes in the local area. This was a revolutionary plan that was considered ahead of its time. The proposal was announced in the local paper but had to be put on hold until after the war. The council didn't have the manpower, the resources or the money to act on their plan straight away, but this project meant that men would have work when they returned from the front after the war's end.

The Easter Rising

Although Ulster had a mainly Unionist population and wanted to remain part of Britain, many other areas of Ireland felt differently. Many people in the south of the country felt that Britain had turned her back on them and they were treated like second-class citizens. Their belief was not unfounded as there were plenty of English laws that discriminated against the Irish. During Easter week in 1916, there was an uprising that would change the face of Irish politics forever. On 24 April, while British forces were fighting in Europe in the war, the Irish Republican Brotherhood began their rebellion against the British government. Their plan was to establish a Republic of Ireland and leave the United Kingdom

Sean Healy, at 13 years old the youngest casualty during the Easter Rising on the Republican side, 1916.

by force. The rising had been planned since the beginning of the war with the hope of gaining the support of Germany for an independent Ireland. With the war raging, Germany was not very supportive despite being offered help by the Brotherhood. The Brotherhood offered Germany access to Britain through Ireland, which they declined. They had planned to help the German forces land in the west of Ireland while the rebels attacked Dublin. The hope was that the British forces would shift focus to Dublin and allow the German forces to secure the River Shannon. The Germans did support the idea of an independent Ireland, but they decided against the rebels' plans. They did send weapons to Ireland before the rising began but the British intercepted the ship before it landed in Ireland. Even this level of treachery planned by the Brotherhood was too much for the Germans! Yet this would not stop those who were hungry for the victory, so the rebellion was planned and put into action. The council that was formed as part of the rising had kept everything secret. They believed that there were members of their own organizations who would attempt to thwart the rising.

More than 1,000 men and women marched through the streets of Dublin. Key positions were attacked in the city as the rebels fought for the independence of Ireland. Even though the British forces were engaged mainly in France at this time, there were still many military units in Ireland. Some were training, some had a brief break from the fighting at the front, and some were recovering from injuries and illness. When the British government was informed of what was happening, they sent thousands of troops to Ireland instead of to the front in Europe. Martial law was declared as the city descended into chaos. The central holding of Britain in Ireland was Dublin Castle and the rebels attacked but failed to take the building. In other areas such as the Jacob's Biscuit factory, the rebels attacked civilians who dared to help the British forces to disband the rebel posts. The British forces were not much better than the rebels, as civilians were shot on more than one occasion out of anger. Trenches were dug in the streets of Dublin. Transport and communications were partially cut off. Streets were barricaded by carts, and citizens were attacked when they tried to dismantle them.

By the middle of the week, the rebels had only secured their posts around the city. They had failed to secure any of the ports or train stations that would have been vital to their victory. The British were able to ship more troops to Ireland. This oversight by the rebels allowed the British force to grow to more than 16,000 troops by the end of the week. Soldiers were sent for from Belfast with plenty of men from Newtownards likely to have been in the ranks.

Within six days the entire rebellion was quashed and the leaders were rounded up. The rebels were outmanned and outgunned from the beginning. Once they realized that they could not win, Patrick Pearse (one of their leaders) agreed to an unconditional surrender on Saturday, 29 April. The surrender document read as follows:

> In order to prevent the further slaughter of Dublin citizens, and in the hope of saving the lives of our followers now surrounded and hopelessly outnumbered, the members of the Provisional Government present at headquarters have agreed to an unconditional surrender, and the commandants of the various districts in the City and County will order their commands to lay down arms.

The fighting continued until the next day as the order was spread to other rebel posts in the country.

Civilians were shocked by the carnage that surrounded them. Around 3,500 people were arrested and more than 1,500 were placed in internment camps or prisons. The leaders of the rising were executed after a court martial found them guilty of treason against the British Empire. Although the citizens of Ireland had supported the Home Rule Bill, they did not condone the actions of this small group of people, nor did they approve of the actions of the British forces. While this failed rebellion did not win the support of the Irish people, the British had lost their trust as well. The people of Newtownards considered the uprising to be part of the war and it was seen as an incredibly underhanded tactic to engage in a civil war while Britain's back was turned. It was a war on a Newtownards person's way of life.

Pigeon-hunting

Some confusion arose as men hunting had begun shooting carrier pigeons. The area had a lot of green fields which provided plenty of wild game birds to be hunted for food. Pigeons and pheasants were firm favourites with the local hunters. Unfortunately for the service pigeons, while the ordinary pigeons were being hunted the carrier pigeons were mistaken for fair game. This saw many carrier pigeons and their important messages going missing. As a result the Ministry of Defence issued an order that pigeon-hunting was to cease immediately.

As May began, the town was not as filled with the festivities it would once have been. On May Day in Holywood there were the traditional maypole dances and fair, but then on 2 May Driver George Casey would die of his wounds while in France, and Rifleman James McCullough would die of his wounds in Dublin after he was shot during the Easter Rising.

Rifleman Thomas James Harrison had worked for the Urban Council Gasworks, been a member of the Mill Street Heroes Loyal Orange Lodge and a member of the Ulster Volunteer Force. During his service he was responsible for rescuing many wounded men while coming under enemy fire. His bravery did not go unnoticed and he was awarded the Military Medal in May 1916, making him the first County Down man to receive this honour.

Although many people were given the sad news that their loved ones had died at the front, others discovered that their family members had become prisoners of war. In one curious case, Private William Boal, who served under the alias of William McHugh, was a prisoner of war at Göttingen prisoner-of-war camp. In March 1916, William Boal's wife received a letter from the Crown Princess of Sweden informing her that her husband was in the camp and the princess had been sending him parcels. This situation was not to last as William died of heart failure on 18 May while still in the camp. However, the strange cases do not end there. Rifleman William Smyth of Greenwell Street was a member of the Ulster Volunteer Force before the outbreak of war. When he first enlisted in 1914 he was sent to the front and was injured in the head in March 1915 while in France. Once he had recovered, he was sent to the front again. In May 1915, he was injured again. For the third time he returned to the front but this time it would be his last. On 19 May 1916, at the age of 22, he was killed during an enemy firefight.

While many of the men of Newtownards were serving at the front with others from all over Britain, the war continued on the high seas. On 31 May, the Battle of Jutland took place in the North Sea. This was the biggest naval battle of the war with a great loss of life on both sides. During the battle there were Newtownards men on board two separate ships. On board HMS *Indefatigable* was Stoker First Class David Magee and on board HMS *Invincible* was Stoker First Class John Moreland. Both these men lost their lives on 31 May, the first day of the battle. Each ship carried more than 1,000 men and suffered heavy losses, with only two of the crew surviving from HMS *Indefatigable* and six from HMS *Invincible*.

Lord Kitchener and HMS Hampshire

The man responsible for a lot of the recruitment from Ireland was Lord Kitchener, Secretary of State for War. On 5 June, Lord Kitchener set off to Russia on HMS *Hampshire* on a diplomatic mission. Shortly before the Battle of Jutland, a U-boat had laid mines off the shores of Orkney in the hope of sinking some British navy ships. On the day that Lord Kitchener set out, the winds were at gale-force level. The belief was that the weather conditions would prevent U-boats being active in the area. So although enemy submarines were not considered a threat, the British did not know about the mines that had been laid a few days earlier. The ship hit a mine between the bows and bridge, and sank within twenty minutes of the detonation. The poor weather made escaping the stricken vessel virtually impossible as lifeboats smashed against the ship. Only twelve of those on board survived the sinking and made it to shore. Among the 737 dead were Lord Kitchener and all ten men of his entourage on the mission.

At the front

During an attack on the German trenches on 26 June, Corporal Jack Peake defied expectations by capturing two German prisoners and searching several trenches while under heavy shellfire. Not only were his actions considered incredibly brave, but he was able to retrieve information that was vital for the first day of the Battle of the Somme, which was due to take place on 1 July 1916. For his efforts he was awarded the Military Medal.

Appeals for the soldiers continued but with less vigour than in the previous fund-raising. The town seemed an empty shell of what it once had been as news of the dead continued to pour in. Nobody appeared to be putting any effort into anything within the town. Countless women dressed in their mourning clothes continuously as a sign of respect for the dead. Up until this point there had been more than 180 men connected with Newtownards and the surrounding townlands who had died during the war, but things were about to get so much worse for the families of the Ards Peninsula. Little did they realize, as they began the celebrations for July with Orange Lodge parades through the town and the beating of the Lambeg drums, that their fathers, brothers and sons were preparing for the bloodiest battle of the war.

The Battle of the Somme

In the old-style calendar, the Battle of the Boyne was fought on 1 July 1690. The anniversary of the battle in 1916 was also the first day of the Battle of the Somme. This date would have been on the mind of any Orange Lodge members at the front on that day. The Battle of the Somme is described by many as the 'bloodiest day in the history of the British army' as the allied loss of life was so great. It was particularly bad for the families of Newtownards as many of the local men who enlisted were there on that fateful day. Many of the Irish forces were placed there for the battle, including the 36th (Ulster) Division. They were ordered to attack

Hand-made cards for the troops.

the Schwaben Redoubt (a German strongpoint in the Somme sector) and advance the allied line. During the previous week, the Germans had been under heavy allied shellfire but with little effect.

On the morning of the attack, it was rumoured that commanding officers clutched at their Orange Lodge sashes. They shouted 'No surrender!' at the top of their voices as they and their

James Dorrian of Talbot Street, Newtownards. Killed on the first day of the Battle of the Somme.

men went over the top. However, the divisions were too quick to advance and they began to come under fire from those who were advancing behind them at a slower pace. In total, 130 Newtownards men lost their lives on the first day alone. The Lewis gun team that was attached to 'B' Company of the 13th Battalion of the Royal Irish Rifles was one of the many teams badly affected by loss of life. The team was given orders to advance to the German trenches, but only three men survived the mission and all were injured. The tight-knit groups of men were no match for the German machine guns and they were quickly mown down by the rapid fire.

Many of the men who died were listed as serving with the 36th (Ulster) Division but not the regiment to which they were attached. One such man was Rifleman George Burns who was from the town and served with the 36th (Ulster) Division. He, like many others, had trained in the Clandeboye camp. Also from the 36th (Ulster) Division was Lance Corporal Alexander Campbell who had been a labourer before the war.

Another regiment that was badly affected was the Royal Irish Rifles,

Robert McCartney, killed on the first day of the Battle of the Somme. Robert was married to Susanna. Susanna also lost her her brother, James Dorrian, on the same day.

to which the 36th (Ulster) Division was attached. Rifleman John McIlveen and his brother William both found themselves on the front line on the first day of the Battle of the Somme with others from the Royal Irish Rifles. For one of the brothers, the war was to end here as John McIlveen was killed in action on the first day. The men who died on this day were not just soldiers; before the war they all had jobs and families. Sergeant Samuel DeVoy was known to many in the town as Sammy. He had been a draper's assistant before the war began. Private John Dornan had been a carpenter. Rifleman John Dorrian had been a factory clerk. Rifleman James Fisher had been a shop assistant and had left behind a wife and two small children.

It is also important to remember the age of some of the men who died on this day. Although the age range was large, many of them were young men who had yet to begin their lives properly. Rifleman John Irvine Hamilton was just 21 years old, and Lance Corporal William James McCoy was even younger at the age of 19. Rifleman Robert McKibbin was a Donaghadee man aged 26. Private William John Melville could be considered an older gentleman when he was killed at the age of 34.

The men who were part of the 36th (Ulster) Division had trained in Clandeboye camp in preparation for the war. Many of the men who had trained there were considered to have less than adequate training. Their career soldier counterparts believed that they would not be able to deal with the battles and probably lacked the ability to follow orders. Despite this, Rifleman Thomas Harrison had been awarded the Military Medal in May 1916. He was still on active service with the Royal Irish Rifles when he was sent to the Somme. He, like so many others, lost his life on the first day of the battle and never had the honour of receiving his medal. It was later presented to his parents.

Lieutenant Colonel Lawrence Arthur Hind, known as Lawrie, was born in England but had married a young woman from County Down. His wife Nina and her family were of great prominence in Northern Ireland. His father-in-law was the Right Hon. Thomas Andrews; his mother-in-law was the sister of Lord William James Pirrie. Lord Pirrie was one of the partners of the Harland and Wolff shipyard in Belfast. His brother-in-law was Thomas Andrews, the chief designer of the *Titanic,* who had died when the ship sank on her maiden voyage across the Atlantic. After the wedding the couple moved to England as Lawrie was a serving soldier with the Sherwood Foresters. He had previously been wounded during the war and had made a full recovery. During the first day of the Battle of the Somme he was killed by an enemy sniper as he attempted to get through to the German trenches. Within five years Nina had lost both her brother and her husband to tragic circumstances. For his efforts, Lawrie was awarded the Military Cross.

One of the important businesses in the town was the Ards Weaving Co. Ltd. The company was owned by Richard Thomas, with three of his sons working with him. One son had migrated to Canada some years before, but had returned when war broke out. Captain (Pilot) Gilbert Watson Webb had been flying over enemy lines to map out trenches and the land when he was hit by enemy gunfire. As he died, his co-pilot was forced to make a crash-landing behind enemy lines, was badly injured and taken prisoner.

The men who took part in this battle would never be seen again and their bodies were never recovered. There were those who had died and were initially considered missing in action. Because many of the bodies could not be recovered, their commanding officers could not be sure who had died and who was missing. It would take time for news of the men's deaths to be confirmed to their families. The British forces lost around 60,000 men on the first day of the battle alone. Of this number, more than 130 of them were Newtownards men.

As the sun rose on the second day of the battle, more Newtownards men would lose their lives, although the death toll would not be as dramatic as on the day before. Because the intensity of the battle, the numbers of men being killed and many more injured, it would have been impossible for the remaining troops to gather all the wounded from the first day's fighting. There were men who were listed as dead or being killed in action on 2 July 1916 who were present at the Battle of the Somme but may have died the day before, or they may have lain wounded since the first day and succumbed to their injuries after not receiving immediate medical help. The Royal Irish Rifles could not get to their wounded soldiers due to the level of fighting, which prevented them making a dash to the injured men. The first two days of the Battle of the Somme were by far the bloodiest with a terribly high death rate. Although the first two days were now over, the death toll continued to rise as the battle raged on and those who had been severely wounded would succumb to their injuries.

The summer of 1916 would see a failure of the wheat harvest in parts of England and Scotland, leading to a bread shortage in Britain. After the Great Famine of Ireland, people were prepared in the event of crops failing. However, the issue was not just with the crops failing but the inability to import food from outside Britain. It was impossible to have food imported from Europe as the continent was already experiencing a massive famine. The British government was greatly concerned about this crop failure as grain supplies previously brought in from the Black Sea area had been blocked by the Turks who had allied themselves to Germany. By this stage of the conflict, more than 80,000 people had starved to death with no signs of food relief getting

Thomas Andrews,
Comber
1873 - 1912

Thomas Andrew who was from Comber.

to the country any time soon. This would prompt the British government to begin plans for food rationing as shortages grew increasingly likely.

As the nights grew darker, the town remained in darkness. To save fuel the lamps were not lit and windows had their blackout curtains drawn. The threat of the German zeppelins' bombing campaign in England frightened everyone to the point where they didn't dare light the lamps outside in case they should draw attention to the area. The aerial bombing from zeppelins had been restricted to England, mainly London, at this point. The main concern for people were the rumours that these aircraft were silent. If a zeppelin did appear over Newtownards, no one would know until it was too late. If Ireland was to be attacked, there was a greater risk of Dublin or Belfast being targeted, but no one took the chance of alerting a zeppelin over residential areas, regardless of where they lived.

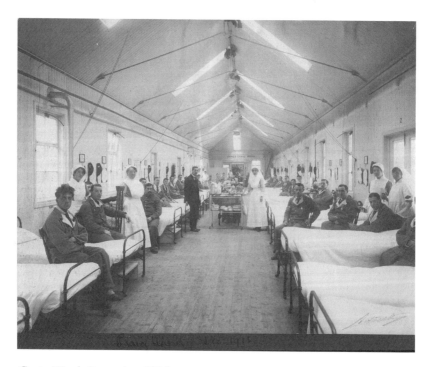

Craig Ward, December 1916.

The gigantic ship sinks

In 1914, the Harland and Wolff shipyard in Belfast had launched the third and final *Olympic*-class liner, the *Britannic*. It was rumoured that the ship was originally named *Gigantic* and the name was later changed, but it may have been a nickname given by the shipbuilders as she was the largest of the trio of liners. In 1915, she was requisitioned as a hospital ship for the duration of the war. Like her sister ship *Titanic*, her career on the sea was to be short-lived. On 21 November 1916, HMHS (His Majesty's Hospital Ship) *Britannic* struck a mine just after 8.00 am while navigating around Kea Island in Greece. Of the 1,066 people on board the ship, only 30 lives were lost. Although this was not the largest tragedy to occur at sea during the war, the *Britannic* was the largest ship to be sunk by the enemy.

Before the bells could sound at midnight to signal the end of another year, another man would die. On 31 December, Rifleman John Harvey would be the last man from Newtownards to die in 1916.

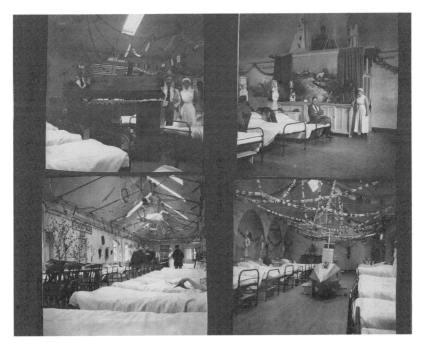

Christmas 1916 at the UVF hospital.

CHAPTER FOUR

1917: Seeing it Through

Another Christmas and New Year had come and gone in the town while the men were fighting at the front. During the festive period, food had been voluntarily rationed by the families of Ards, but now rationing of food and clothing was going to be a harsh reality until the war was over. The general public had initially believed that the war would only last a few weeks or perhaps a few months at most. Nobody had expected it to continue for more than a year. Now there seemed to be no end in sight.

The Central Powers had announced that any ship they came across was now fair game to be torpedoed and sunk. Any ship could potentially be the target of an enemy U-boat. In the past, the Rules of War had dictated that only warships could engage each other, but now it did not matter whether it was a passenger ship full of civilians, a warship full of soldiers or a hospital ship full of sick and dying men. This change of tactics came about because mainland Europe was suffering from massive famines. The enemy was hoping that preventing ships from transporting goods would expose Britain to the same food shortages as the rest of Europe. The end game was to cause most of the population to starve to death. Thousands of people had suffered and died from famine across the European community. What the Central Powers didn't realize about Britain was the vast scale of the farming communities. Britain could easily survive without food being imported into the country, especially Ireland. Ireland had already suffered from the potato famine around 100 years earlier and was now prepared for any type of food shortages. Since the famine, farmers had ensured that there was a wide variety in their crops and any signs of blight on their farms were dealt with swiftly.

It was too risky to import or export goods anywhere, and even the short journey across the Irish Sea was deemed dangerous. This would lead to all cross-channel trade being officially recommended to stop until the end of the war, although businesses still wanted to continue as normal and people still needed to earn a wage. However, the risk was too great for civilians to take, now that any boat could be attacked by a submarine. The fishermen who worked on the Irish Sea were faced with a problem of where to fish, but all was not lost. When viewed from above, it is easy to see that the lough can be easily protected. Strangford Lough is surrounded by a peninsula and is connected directly to the Irish Sea. The only way for a submarine to get into the lough is through a small inlet, between the villages of Strangford and Portaferry, known as the Strangford Bar. The tide within the lough is known to be unpredictable and to move incredibly quickly. Parts of the lough are incredibly shallow and the mud flats in the lough near Newtownards become exposed during low tides. If a German submarine was to attempt an attack from here, it could find itself becoming stranded very quickly and those inside would be at the mercy of the locals.

The lough itself was not the only place that was considered dangerous for outsiders. Around the Ards Peninsula there are several rocky reefs. These offshore half-tide reefs have been responsible for countless sinkings and without knowing where they were, the enemy put themselves in danger. One of the first vessels that could spot a U-boat entering the lough was the Strangford Ferry. The ferry service between the towns of Strangford and Portaferry has been in place for hundreds of years. This small boat was responsible for maintaining quick contact between the towns at the end of the peninsula and the rest of the county. Without the ferry, it can take around an hour and a half to drive from Portaferry to Strangford, even in a modern car. The ferry takes only twenty minutes to transport people across the lough.

Although the waters were choppy and incredibly dangerous because of the undertow, the locals knew there was plenty of fish and shellfish available. Even a boy with a rod or a net could easily catch some dinner. This solved the problem of what people could eat, but it didn't help the fisherman who relied on fishing as their trade. From this point on, anyone who decided to venture into the Irish Sea to fish would be taking their life in their hands.

Series of postcards depicting the fall of the Axis forces.

Fishing was not the only maritime activity to be disrupted. Travelling across the water was considered dangerous for citizens. The Dowager Marchioness of Londonderry was not able to travel from England to attend the annual meeting with the Mothers' Union. The meeting was held in Londonderry Schoolhouse, and the branch secretary read a letter from the marchioness expressing her desire to be there. In her letter, she acknowledged that the mothers of Newtownards had helped with every possible war charity. She also stated that the Mothers' Union worked hard at bringing people together, despite the divisions, 'in the one great bond of motherhood'.

Voluntary rationing was actively encouraged across Britain from this point on and allotments were made available for people to grow their own vegetables. The allotments in Newtownards were quickly taken by people who shared the workload. It was not uncommon for neighbours to help tend each other's plots and share their vegetables. Small yards and windowsills became packed with pots and planters of the finest natural produce. There were so many vegetables being grown in Newtownards that people were able to share with others outside the town. Regular donations of fresh vegetables were made to the army training camps and naval bases, as well as the regular woollen goods and cigarettes that were requested by soldiers. The use of natural resources didn't end with people fishing in the lough and growing their own food. The roads that lead out to the farms and the countryside were packed with wild berry bushes. Children could often be seen collecting delicious wild blackberries on Sunday mornings after church and Sunday school. Little girls were often scolded for ruining their Sunday skirts and dresses by carrying berries home in them. This abundance of natural resources has been available to the locals since the first settlements appeared and now people planned to use those resources once again as did the first settlers.

One of the most-used and readily-available ingredients was the humble apple. 'Lady Edith' ran the household column in the *Belfast Newsletter* and gave tips to help in running the home. In one column, she responded to a question about apple pulp and the ways in which it could be used. The emphasis was on preserving ingredients for as long as possible and the best thing for apple pulp was sugar. Once a batch of apple pulp had been made, it could be used for months to make pies, tarts or even a soufflé. The column was one of the best places for women to get information about cooking on rations and inspiration for meals. There were plenty of suggestions for meatless meals that contained a variety of vegetables to help bulk them out.

Food was not the only thing being rationed. Petrol was also heavily rationed across the country. This was a major problem for people who lived in the rural areas. The rail network stretched from Belfast city to Newtownards town centre. From here, it split off and travelled down the country through Comber and to Donaghadee. The line stopped at Donaghadee and didn't travel any further down the peninsula. This meant that the only way to travel around the peninsula was by car or bus. The petrol rationing limited cars from driving down the peninsula and forced more people to take the country buses. The rumours and reports of rowdy young women on the buses going to work in the mills became so bad that the local papers picked up the story.

The year had got off to a particularly bad start for two men from Comber. On 16 January, Charles Kelly assaulted the station-master of Comber train station. David Johnston, the station-master, was attacked with an iron bar. Mr Johnston had become a local hero the year before, after he saved a man from an oncoming train. He was not hurt in the attack but Charles Kelly was arrested and sentenced to prison. It was believed that the two men had a disagreement and Mr Kelly decided that the best way to end it was by assaulting Mr Johnston.

January also saw a new-found vigour in fund-raising for the troops. The British Red Cross organized a dance fund-raiser in St Andrews Hall in Comber. People were encouraged to join together to raise funds for the boys at the front. Soldiers who had been lucky enough to get home leave or were in the local hospital recovering from injuries joined the party to help raise spirits. People danced and cheered in the hall as they celebrated with the troops. Those who were still at the front continued to write home to their loved ones. Men wrote home to their mothers and told them of the horrible weather that they were enduring at the front. As the numbers of sick, wounded and dead men continued to rise, it was clear that something was needed to help relieve the pressure on the troops. One of the things that helped the men at the front was the formation of the Women's Auxiliary Corps. The formation of the corps was designed to relieve the men of 'soft jobs' such as working in the stores, transport and on the army bases. Having women in these roles freed up more able-bodied men and allowed them to fight at the front.

Scandal was discovered across the country when it was revealed that some landlords had been increasing their tenants' rents. Under the Increase of Rent and Mortgage Interest (War Restrictions) Act 1915, rent increases and charges were not to be imposed on tenants during the war. The Act was put in place to protect tenants during the war, after landlords attempted to capitalize on the surge of people who came to Glasgow at the beginning of the conflict. It is unclear why the landlords decided to increase their rents as they were already being watched in case any were potentially hiding spies in short-term lease properties.

Mr Johnston, Comber station-master.

Aftermath of the Easter Rising

David Lloyd George had been appointed prime minister of the wartime coalition government at the end of 1916. In March 1917, he announced that he would begin talks in Ireland. The rebellion during Easter the year before had shown exactly how desperate Ireland was to govern herself. This event would be known in Irish history as the 'Easter Rising'. Unlike the prime ministers that preceded him, David Lloyd George was prepared to discuss the future of Ireland. He understood that most of Ireland wanted to be free from British rule, but the north of Ireland wished to remain with Britain. The death and destruction that took place during the Easter Rising had left a bad taste in people's mouths. Even though the war was still raging across Europe, it

Newtownards Railway Station.

Signal box, Comber train station.

Railway crest.

A train approaches the station in Comber.

A steam engine stops at Comber train station.

had been decided that the talks should begin as soon as possible. Parliament did not want to run the risk of another rebellion in Ireland while most of the army was in the trenches. One of the biggest fears of the British government was the Central Powers offering to help the rebels. The war was becoming unreadable and desperate. If the Central Powers convinced the Irish rebels to join them, Ireland would be consumed by civil war and become the new front line. If Ireland should be taken, the war would then be lost for the allies.

At around the same time, it was announced that Ireland would not be included in conscription to the army. Up to this point the armed forces had relied on men volunteering to enlist. However, Britain was now at the stage where every man who wanted to enlist had already done so. The death toll and list of injured men continued to climb higher and higher and the number of troops available for the front line was steadily decreasing. The government had deemed it necessary to bring the Military Service Act into force the year before, but it was not until a year later that it was confirmed that Ireland would not be included. The men of Newtownards continued to enlist, regardless of the dangers that they would face. Although Ireland was not included in conscription, Newtownards men felt obliged to enlist as their English counterparts were drafted.

Before Christmas, Rifleman John Ledgerwood had been injured while serving with the Royal Irish Rifles, resulting in his requiring multiple surgery. Although the operations seemed successful, he later died on 6 January 1917. As his family dealt with the pain that comes from losing a son, they were to be dealt another blow only a few weeks later. John's brother, Rifleman Samuel Hugh Ledgerwood, had been missing in action since the first day of the Battle of the Somme. By the end of January 1917, the family would have confirmation that he had been killed in action.

After being awarded the Military Medal in June 1916 for his bravery, Corporal Jack Peake was sent to the front for the first day of the Battle of the Somme, since when he had been posted as missing in action. His family did not get the confirmation of his death until January 1917. His father John was employed by Lord Dunleath as a carpenter on the Dunleath estate. Jack's medal was presented to his mother in a ceremony that was attended by Lady Dunleath. This would be the beginning of a flood of bad news. It had been difficult to confirm who had been killed and who was missing after the Battle of the Somme. Many of the families had received news that their loved ones were simply missing, but this was about to change. As further news began to trickle back home regarding the men missing from the Somme, it was not to end with just one or two men. Lance Corporal James McNeilly was another soldier from the Royal Irish Rifles who had been missing since that day. By February 1917, it had been confirmed to his family that he had died at the front. Casualties from the Battle of the Somme and the Battle of Verdun amounted to more than 1.7 million men, a number that was heavily criticized by the general public in Britain and France. People believed this death toll to be inexcusable considering that the lines were still at a deadlock. It was simply not good enough. Hundreds of men from Newtownards had died at the Somme and there was a public demand that there should not be such a large loss of life again.

America joins the war

On 6 April, the entire dynamic of the war changed as America joined the allies in the conflict. Up to this point they had decided to remain neutral, but as Germany had begun targeting any vessel that they considered to be a threat, they had a change of heart. The perceived threat from the allies was so great that the U-boats had begun sinking ships that were flying a neutral flag. Up until then, the war had been known as 'the European War'. Now with America involved it had officially become a 'world war'. The conflict had been on the minds of many Americans since the sinking of the *Lusitania* but the politicians had downplayed the tragedy as a mistake. The announcement that any ship that could be a threat *would* be attacked changed everything. Any ship was now a target and this could mean the loss of innocent American lives.

America was quick to pull her forces together and rapidly promoted recruitment. This allowed men who had moved from Ireland to America a chance to join the war. Up till now, there had been a few men from Newtownards who had moved to Canada and America who had been at the front. Most of the men had travelled back from America to Ireland in order to enlist and fight in their local regiments. Many of these young men had come from low-income families and had moved away in the hope of making their fortunes in the land of the free.

The North Down Ladies' Choir held a fund-raiser for the British Red Cross after hearing about the injured soldiers from the front. They were distraught after they learned what was happening across Europe. As the German forces were retreating, they had adopted a scorched earth policy. This meant that every possible natural resource was to be destroyed, including the water supplies, which were poisoned. Any German soldiers who were captured were put to work as stretcher-bearers and carried the wounded British troops. Fund-raising for the troops had become much more than just sending tobacco and knitted items to the front: these women were trying to help the men survive the German retreat.

The hybrid tea roses

Alexander Dixon II and his family were breeding roses in the Dixon Rose Nursery (known at the time as Dixons of Hawlmark) and this year would see them unveil their new roses. A red hybrid tea rose named 'Kitchener of Khartoum' was bred and named in honour of Lord Kitchener. The 'Kootenay' rose was a lighter pink and cream rose. A canary-yellow rose named 'Ulster Gem' was created by Alexander's uncle Hugh. The family had been breeding roses in Newtownards since 1836, after they emigrated from Scotland. These roses were part of a long line of award-winning flowers. 'Kitchener of Khartoum' was a Royal National Rose Society Gold Medal winner and the names showed the town's support for Britain and the desire to remain part of Britain.

As the months rolled on, news from the Somme continued to come in. Private William John Dalzell had been missing in action since the first day of the Battle of the Somme. It was only in May 1917 that news finally reached home of what had happened to him. It was believed that he had been killed in action on the day that he went missing. The same news reached another family of the town at the same time. Lance Corporal George Mahaffey was originally from America and had settled in Newtownards when he was married. Rifleman Robert McCartney's family also received the news of his death, along with Rifleman Daniel McCutcheon. David Gamble's family had been informed in December that their son was a prisoner in a PoW camp after he had been injured on the first day of the Battle of the Somme. However, the small hope that they might see their son again was extinguished when they received the news of his death. He had died months earlier on 8 July 1916, at the age of 17. During the few days of his capture he had died of his wounds while being held by the Germans.

Attack in the harbour

Although the lough and inside the peninsula was considered a dangerous place by the locals and an idiotic place for the enemy to attempt to navigate into for an attack, it didn't stop U-boats from patrolling the other side of the peninsula. On 2 May, U-boat *UC 65* attacked four boats in Ballyhalbert harbour in the Irish Sea. The *St. Mungo*, *Derrymore*, *Amber* and the *Morion* were all transporting goods when they were attacked without warning. The *Amber* was scuttled around 2 miles from the bay and the *Morion* was scuttled around 4 miles from the bay. All the members of those crews survived. Only some of the crew from the *Derrymore* survived. The U-boat was captained by Otto Steinbrinck, one of the most respected captains of the German fleet. The crew of the Cloughey lifeboat, *The John*, were on hand to rescue the survivors of the U-boat attacks.

Despite the attacks on the outer side of the peninsula, it was summer as normal for the local Scout groups. After the Easter camp at the Smyth Farm in Dundonald, the summer camp was held at Cross Island in Comber. Cross Island is more commonly known as Lighthouse Island because of the lighthouse that once stood there. Between 1715 and 1884, the lighthouse was a beacon for passing ships on Cross Island, but when a new lighthouse was erected on Mew Island in 1884 the older lighthouse was abandoned. Although the Scouts liked to camp there in the summertime, the islands were once known to be a smugglers' hotspot. It is not known when the smugglers stopped using the islands to bring tobacco and spirits into County Down but it is believed that they were still being used in the early part of the twentieth century. If the Scouts had done any travelling around the area, they would have had the opportunity to see a local tourist attraction if they had ventured to Portaferry. For more than 150 years, the Whale's Jawbone Arch stood beside a house and attracted visitors from far and wide.

The Whale's Jawbone Arch

Shift in Irish politics

June would see another change in Irish politics and the various political parties. Sinn Féin had emerged as a new party to help lead Ireland into the new era of Home Rule. In July 1917, the Irish Convention opened as a way to help decide how the future of Ireland would take shape after the war. The convention was held in Regent House, Dublin. The idea behind the convention was to discuss the best way to grant self-government to Ireland. However, this meeting of the political parties was highly flawed from the beginning. The new Sinn Féin party had its own ideas about Home Rule and had plenty of support from Nationalists. Most of the Irish Labour Movement refused to attend the convention and take part in the deliberations. The only members of the Irish Labour Movement who did attend were the Belfast delegates. The Ulster Unionists who attended the convention were rigid in their views and refused to compromise on anything. This led to them alienating any allies that they had in left in the opposing parties.

Forming the IRA

Up till now, the Nationalist forces had come under a blanket term of the Irish Nationalists or Irish Volunteers. However, this year would see the formation of a group familiar to most people, the IRA. The Irish Republican Army was formed with the belief that Ireland should be an independent republic and that political violence was the only way to achieve it. The formation was also in response to the UVF gun-running and threat of violence from 1914. Over the years, the group would grow, change and have several breakaway factions. This initial group of soldiers would be recognized as the first official army of Ireland and would later be known as the Irish Defence Forces. The IRA that most people are familiar with was formed a few years later, after the War of Independence in Ireland when they renounced the treaty between Britain and Ireland.

Comber Whiskey

Comber Whiskey was a local favourite in the public houses of the working men. Until 1917, Comber Whiskey was a family business owned by the Bruce family. Samuel Bruce had bought the distillery in 1871 when the previous owners decided to retire. Since 1914, the distillery had been producing less and less whiskey as demand fell. During 1917, Samuel Bruce had been meeting with some gentlemen who had an interest in the business. By the end of the year the Bruce family had sold its share of the company to a group of Belfast businessmen. This would be the beginning of the end for Comber Whiskey. The market had changed and people preferred blended whisky to the pure pot-still whiskey from the small town.

A year had passed since the Battle of the Somme when more than 100 Newtownards men had lost their lives. Many of those who had been listed as missing in action since then were finally confirmed as killed in action. Lance Corporal James Dorrian was a labourer before he left for the war. The news that he was not missing in action but confirmed as killed in action was the beginning of a stream of bad news for families throughout June and July 1917. American troops had arrived in France in June and helped to strengthen the front. With the reinforcements coming from America, the allied forces were able to push forward. On 7 June, around twenty huge mines exploded under the German trenches and signalled the beginning of the Battle of Messines. For months beforehand, the allies had been mining under the German lines with the intention of setting off a series of massive explosions. The explosions were so loud it was claimed that they could be heard in London. The German forces realized too late that they were under attack and began to shell the empty British trenches. The 36th (Ulster) Division was one of the units that crossed no man's land to the German trenches. When they arrived they found more than 10,000 dead German soldiers and thousands more wounded or in shock from the mine attack. The 10th (Irish) Division found themselves in the same position as their Ulster counterparts. The allied forces made quick work of rounding up what remained of the German troops before the bigger Battle of Ypres.

While many people celebrated the final break in the deadlock, others received news about their loved ones. Corporal Edward Bennett was one of the many soldiers whose death was confirmed. Private Edward Adair and Rifleman Robert Hugh Allen had both been missing for a year when their families finally received confirmation that they had been killed in action the year before. Rifleman William Angus had gone missing on the first day of the Battle of the Somme and his family would also only now receive the news that he had been killed in action the year before. Rifleman William George Kelly had been a weaver before the war and Rifleman William McQuiston had been a house-painter.

Many of these families had hoped that their loved ones were just missing and hoped that soon they would hear that they had been found safe and well. Sergeant Alfred Blythe had been missing since the first day of the Battle of the Somme and his family still hoped that he was alive. As news trickled in that others who had been missing were now confirmed as killed in action, Alfred's family received news of a different kind. In a Scottish newspaper there had been a photo printed of the prisoners at Gefangenenlager, Schneidemuhl, near Posen in Silesia. One of the prisoners had lost his memory, did not know his name and his regiment was unknown, but his features made the people of Newtownards think that he may have been the missing Sergeant Blythe. Sadly, this was not the case as his family would later receive the news that he had been killed in action on 1 July 1916. Rifleman Archibald Thomas Campbell was serving with the Royal Irish Rifles at the same time as his father was serving with the Royal Garrison Artillery. Archibald had been reported as missing in action after the first day of the Battle of the Somme but it was a year later that his family received the news that he had died. His father James Campbell had died only three months earlier and never knew what had become of his son.

In July, Edward Carson addressed a crowd in Belfast about the peace talks to end the war. The latest German chancellor, Georg Michaelis, had made a speech claiming that Germany's current submarine warfare campaign was not in violation of any human rights, it was only intended to make an impact on Britain's economy. Edward Carson's response to the speech was that it was 'hollow'. Carson also said

Sir Edward Carson.

that the peace-loving people of Britain would be ready to hold peace talks when Germany withdrew her troops from the occupied countries. He spoke of a peace that would bring back the men, a lasting peace, and that the men who would not come home would not have died in vain. At this point the German chancellor was still confident of Germany's success in the war and said the allied forces had a 'lust for conquest'. Only a few weeks before, King George V had issued a proclamation changing the name of the Royal Family from the historic Saxe-Coburg-Gotha to the House of Windsor as the German connections and the attitude of the German government made a lot of people uncomfortable. King George renounced all names and ties with Germany after daylight air-raids had killed eighteen children.

Attack on the *Belgian Prince*

Off the island of Troy, a shipping route to America can be found, something that the German forces knew only too well. Harry Hassan, who was born in Bangor in County Down, was the captain of the *Belgian Prince* cargo ship as she steamed from Liverpool to Virginia with a shipment of blue clay. The ship was approximately 175 miles from Troy Island off the north-west coast of Ireland when she encountered a U-boat. As the ship was steaming forward, she was torpedoed by *U-55* under the command of *Oberleutnant zur See* Wilhelm Werner. The crew was able to abandon the ship and everyone made it to a lifeboat safely. When the ship had been hit, her communications were knocked out and they could not signal for help or rescue. As the three lifeboats were in the water, the U-boat surfaced and shelled the ship. Once they had finished attacking the ship, they ordered the crew of the *Belgian Prince* onto the hull of the U-boat. Captain Hassan was taken below while the crew was searched for weapons. As they stood on top of the U-boat, their lifebelts were taken from them and they could only watch as their lifeboats were destroyed. What happened next has been described by many as an act of murder. When the crew of *U-55* was satisfied that the crew of the *Belgian Prince* was defenceless, they went below decks and closed the hatch. The crew of the *Belgian Prince* was left standing on top of the U-boat with no lifebelts, no lifeboats and more than 100 miles from the nearest shoreline as the U-boat went below the surface. The commander of the U-boat is rumoured to have previously sunk other ships and killed their crews in this way. Three members of the crew managed to survive in the cold Atlantic waters and make it to safety. Without them, the story would never have been told. Captain Hassan was never heard of again. It was believed that he became a prisoner at Ruhleben internment camp in Germany but was never seen by his family again.

Corporal James Neil Doggart of the Royal Irish Fusiliers and Rifleman Thomas Maddock Doggart of the Royal Irish Rifles were brothers who in a cruel twist of fate found themselves both at the front on the first day of the Battle of the Somme. In an even crueller twist, both men would also lose their lives on this day on the battlefield. Thomas was believed to be missing in action at first and the news of his death didn't reach his family until July 1917.

News quickly spread through the town that those who had been missing were slowly being confirmed as killed in action. A feeling of dread filled the streets when the postman was on his daily rounds. Children began to spy on the postmen at the beginning of their deliveries to see if they had any 'special brown envelopes' in their bags. If they did, the children would run ahead of them and start knocking on doors to warn people that there was bad news coming.

All Saints' Day

Every year on 1 November, the doors to the Saltwater Brig public house open for the day. The key of the bar was kept behind the doors of the local church. The Saltwater Brig is believed to be one of the oldest working buildings in Ireland. It is rumoured that the building dates back to before 1765 but this date cannot be confirmed. What is certain is that the building was a public house for more than 200 years. The tradition of opening the Brig on All Saints' Day continued until the 1970s. Despite the political conflict, many people still joined together on the day to pray for their loved ones and that they would have reached heaven if they didn't get to come home.

The dark autumn evenings meant having to put gas lamps on in the houses. The Comber Gas Light Company decided it would

Looking down the tracks at Comber train station.

The train station, Comber.

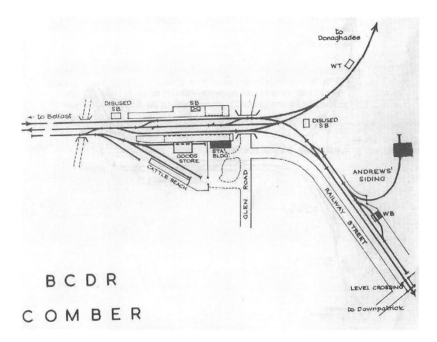

Map of the rail system in Comber.

be a good idea to put up the price of gas in the town for the public gas lamps. Their plan was to increase the rate from 5s 9d per 1,000 cubic feet to 7s 6d per 1,000 cubic feet. There was a public uproar at the thought of such an increase during a time of conflict. The town quickly pulled together and staged a mass protest outside the Comber Gas Light Company building. It was then decided in a meeting with the managing director that the cost was too much for the taxpayer and the town. The agreed price ended up at 6s 8d per 1,000 cubic feet and would not exceed that.

    After boats had been sunk near Ballyhalbert earlier in the year, crews were more vigilant about U-boat activity. On Christmas Eve, the SS *Daybreak* was torpedoed without warning as she was transporting maize. John Bailie of Newcastle townland was the boat contractor attending the South Rock Lightship. Part of his contract was that if the crew was short-handed he would remain on board. He described seeing the loss of the steamer *Daybreak* on 24 December 1917, 1 mile east of the lightship:

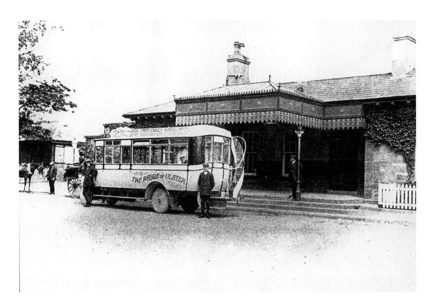

Pride of Ulster bus at Newtownards Railway Station.

I remember being on the South Rock as a temporary, 2s/6d a day and feed yourself. On Christmas Eve 1917 about midday the *Daybreak* loaded with maize was torpedoed and twenty-one were lost. Her nose was cut clean off. It happened so quick her propeller was going round in the air as she sank. You talk about explosions, boilers bursting one after another.

It was reported that she sank within five minutes of being hit. The Cloughey lifeboat was scrambled to save the crew but all twenty-one crew members were lost. The next day HMS *Buttercup* rammed and sank *U-86* in the Irish Sea as it attempted to attack another boat. All forty-four members of the crew were lost.

CHAPTER FIVE

1918: The Final Blows

The Women's Land Army was a civilian organization comprising ladies who worked in the fields to grow food for the local people, replacing the male agricultural workers who had joined the forces. All across Britain there were posters of these women – popularly known as the Land Girls – which helped to encourage everyone to support them and their work. In Newtownards and the peninsula there had been more women living in the area than men before the war, so the area had always had a strong female workforce to support the employment sector. Labourers still travelled from as far as Donegal to work in the area and could receive 25s for a week's work on the farms.

As trade became more difficult as the war continued, the government was forced to impose rationing by law. During 1916 and 1917, Newtownards had been rationing food and clothing voluntarily to help show support for the war effort. This meant that it was not as big a shock and adjustment for people to make, but it did cause a slight panic when rationing had to be legally enforced as there were stricter rules to follow. No longer could you just buy your extra food from the local store if you weren't growing it. With the area being filled with farmland and crops being grown all year round, the farmers now had problems with theft. They would often catch orphaned children stealing cabbages or potatoes from the fields in order to survive. If the unfortunate child was caught, they were not rewarded with sympathy and taken in by a kind individual. The local constable was called and the orphan was taken to the workhouse in the centre of the town. Police were also on the lookout for businesses that might try to overcharge for goods or indulge in racketeering, especially after the scandal of the illegal rent increases the year before. A bread van was caught by Sergeant Duffy as part of a sting operation for selling overpriced bread. Although this case went to court, there was very little done about it. At first it was dismissed but then a fine was issued on appeal. Dixon and Sons of Hawlmark, who were famous for their roses, also sold vegetable seeds. They would regularly post adverts in the papers to remind people when to plant seeds for year-round vegetables and of course remind people that they sold them.

Conscription and Home Rule

In the previous year, it had been announced that conscription to the army would not be enforced in Ireland. However, as the Germans continued to push their offensive and the allied forces continued to lose more men, the British government began to reconsider its stance on the subject. It would be this decision to introduce conscription to Ireland that would shape the future political win for Sinn Féin. At the same time, the Irish Convention was coming to a close. The findings concluded that Ireland could govern herself and that Home Rule would work. This would be applied to most of the country, with six counties in the north to be excluded. These counties were Down, Londonderry, Antrim, Armagh, Tyrone and Fermanagh. The province of Ulster is made up of nine counties but Cavan, Donegal and Monaghan would be included as part of the new Irish Republic. This would be a temporary agreement between Britain and Ireland for five years. When the five-year period was up, the situation would be reviewed and discussed again before a final decision was reached. This was not an ideal situation for any of the British politicians but it was hoped that it would work until after the war was over. After the Easter Rising, the British government wanted to keep the Irish population happy until everything could be settled properly. There was a huge fear that the Nationalists would help the Central Powers if some sort of agreement about the future of Ireland was not reached. One of the biggest problems for the Nationalist population was the fact that it was very scattered in County Down. This made it difficult to get a nominated Nationalist representative into Parliament. Out of the nine seats available, two should have represented the Nationalist minority.

Local news

At the end of January, it was announced that Miss Wilson was to be the new headmistress of the Girls' Model School. Miss Wilson was responsible for bringing multiple awards to her previous school and it was hoped that she would do the same for the Girls' School. While people were celebrating the latest addition to local education, the sudden death of a local hairdresser would shock the town. Joseph Robinson was a hairdresser who worked in Newtownards and was in Belfast when he was suddenly taken ill. He was just outside City Hall when an ambulance had to be called for him. Unfortunately he did not make it to the Royal Victoria Hospital in time. The customers from his North Street shop were shocked

Certificate awarded to Lieutenant Corporal R. Proudfoot of the 36th (Ulster) Division for gallantry and devotion to duty, 15 December 1918.

to hear of his sudden passing. An even greater shock came when a gypsy man assaulted a young girl on 16 February. The gypsy, John Young, was sentenced to six months in prison for this attack.

On 21 March, six more men from the Ards area lost their lives. Among them was Second Lieutenant Edmund De Wind, a local man originally from Comber. He was killed in action after bravely holding his post despite heavy gunfire and being wounded. His bravery and sacrifice were recognized and he was awarded the Victoria Cross. There would also be a street named after him in Comber, De Wind Drive, as a memorial.

While it was tragic that men were injured and dying, it was still considered the 'honourable' thing to do; to die serving your country rather than not serve at all. The Ulster men prided themselves on being fearless and prepared to lay down their lives for their king. So when it became known that some men had disappeared and possibly deserted from the army, there was uproar. S.C. Kelly had

James Robert Armour of Greyabbey

Margaret Armour née Robinson and her son James Alexander Armour

joined the Royal Irish Rifles in April 1916. He was listed in an English paper as a deserter when he disappeared on Christmas Day the year before.

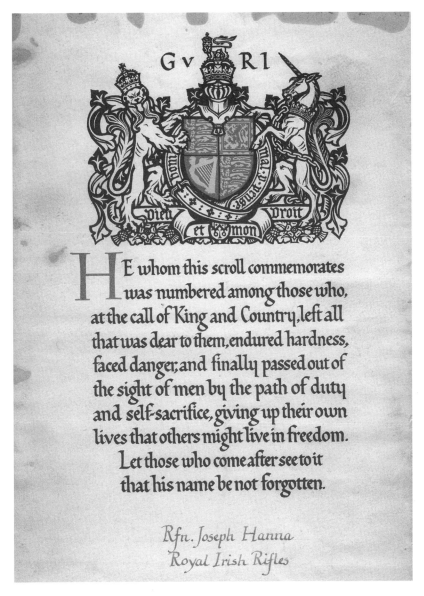

Scroll commemorating Joseph Hanna of the Royal Irish Rifles.

C.S. Lewis

C.S. Lewis, the author famous for his *Chronicles of Narnia* children's books, was born in Belfast in 1898. He began his literary career at Oxford University but had been enrolled in the British army shortly after he had been awarded his scholarship. At the time of his enrolment, he was still under 21 and his father had to countersign his paperwork. He was serving in the trenches when he was injured by British shell fragments which fell short of their target on 15 April 1918, leaving him with broken ribs and superficial wounds. Two of his colleagues were killed in the same blast. It was this injury and the death of his friends that would help to shape his views on warfare, his writing and his relationships for years to come.

Big Changes in Comber

After years of being in the Georgian House in The Square, the Northern Bank in Comber was moving. The new premises would

Women and children going about their daily business on Mill Street, Comber.

Spinning Mill, Comber, Co. Down.

Postcard of Spinning Mill, Comber.

be on the corner of The Square and Killinchy Street. The 12 July celebrations would also be held in Comber this year. The field that hosted the celebrations was owned by Mr Hamilton Coulter of New Comber House. To kick off the July celebrations in Newtownards this year, there would be a horse and sports show with cups, awards and grand prizes awarded to successful entrants.

However, there was a catch to this event in that a horse might be bought by the government to serve as a charger or troop horse. The money offered for such horses was a good amount considering the circumstances. For a charger, there was a fixed fee of £75. For a trooper, there was a fixed fee of £60. The sports day filled with military personnel who tried their hands at different events. The winners had their prizes presented to them by Lady Clanmorris in the absence of Brigadier General Hacket-Pain. This was only the beginning of a new wave of the military reaching out to the public

Comber train station.

for support. The purchased horses needed to be shoed, and the three local barracks (Newtownards, Clandeboye and Ballykinlar) needed men to do it. The successful men would receive a six-month contract with the army at one of the bases.

The railway line ran from Belfast to Newtownards and on to Comber. This left most of the peninsula cut off with no rail service. The Ards Motor Transport announced there would be a change in April to the service that was provided to the peninsula. When the train from Belfast arrived in Newtownards station, a bus would leave at 10.35 am to take passengers to Greyabbey, Portaferry and other towns on the peninsula. It wasn't stated why this change was put in place but there were concerns over the rationing of petrol.

RMS *Carpathia*

RMS *Carpathia* became famous after she saved more than 700 survivors of the *Titanic* from lifeboats after her sinking following an iceberg collision in 1912. Sadly, just like the *Titanic*, the *Carpathia* was also to meet her end in the cold waters of the Atlantic. While off the south-east coast of Ireland on 17 July, the ship was torpedoed twice by U-boat *U-55*. When the ship went down, the passengers took to the lifeboats for safety, only to see the U-boat surface and fire a third torpedo into the stricken vessel. The passengers were terrified by the sight of the enemy submarine and rightly feared for their lives. They were sitting ducks on the open water. It was only the arrival of HMS *Snowdrop* that saved the survivors by opening fire on the submarine and driving it away before it could

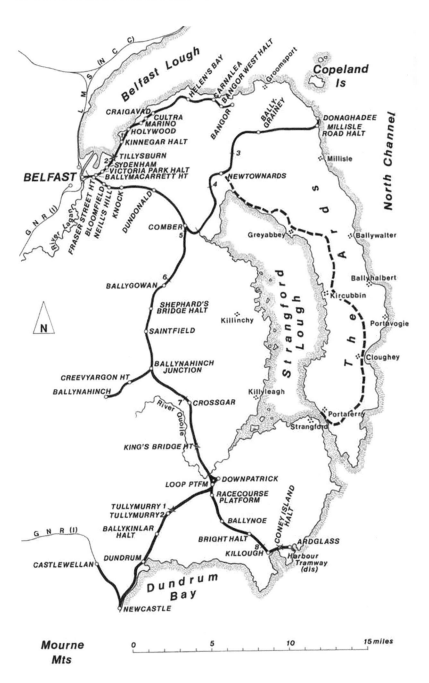

Map of rail tracks during the war.

RMS Carpathia sinking.

kill everyone in the lifeboats. Submarine *U-55* was the same U-boat responsible for the sinking of the *Belgian Prince* and the murder of her crew in 1917. If HMS *Snowdrop* had not arrived when she did, there is a good chance that *Oberleutnant zur See* Wilhelm Werner would have given the command to open fire on the lifeboats to ensure that there were no witnesses to this war crime.

The war had now begun to impact on the interests of farmers and food suppliers in the area. During a meeting in Andrew's Hall in Comber, the Comber Branch of the Ulster Farmers' Union (UFU) was formed. The UFU comprised the largest democratic organization in Ulster representing the interests of farmers and rural life in Parliament.

The viceroy visits

The lord lieutenant of Ireland was Viscount John French, a military man who believed strongly in the conscription of Irish men and peace in Ireland and who paid a visit to Newtownards in August. During the trip up from Dublin, the viceroy was planning to stay with the Marquis of Londonderry at the Mount Stewart estate. After attending to a few engagements in Belfast, the viceroy and his party stopped in Newtownards before travelling further down to Mount Stewart. The town was decorated with bunting and banners for the esteemed guest of honour. During his speech to the town, he spoke of how honoured he was by the welcome and gave high praise to the community. The fund-raising and assistance for the troops that had come from the area had not gone unnoticed.

Ballywhite House in Portaferry was one of the oldest grand houses in the area and it was sold to a branch of the Brownlow family during this year. This was just one of many houses and estates that had to be sold off during the war. In January, Beechgrove in Ballyskeagh had been sold at auction as well. The sales of estates raised the question of what to do with the empty estates of fallen soldiers. Although there was a legal answer, which was to sell such estates at auction, there was the moral question. Should the estates of fallen soldiers be sold to men who were cowards and had stayed behind? Some people believed that it was disrespectful to the dead to sell their property in this way, but no other solution was offered regarding empty houses.

It is hard to believe, but even at this stage of the war heavy recruitment was still taking place. At this point nobody knew how much longer the war might continue and the allies were not prepared to surrender. On 15 September, a huge recruitment rally took place in Conway Square, Newtownards. More than 4,000 people attended the display, despite more than 1,000 men having already joined the colours since the outbreak of war. The hope was that men would sign up voluntarily rather than being conscripted. Lieutenant Colonel Pike spoke to the crowd, telling them that some of the men in his camps had been out at the front lines five times by now. He believed it was time for the men who were left behind to take up the cause. Many of the men who were joining the Ulster divisions were Englishmen and Scotsmen. To Reverend Dr Wright, this was an absolute disgrace to Ulster. He told the crowd that he had seen papers telling of the allies' positions. It wouldn't be long before they would be crossing into the German fatherland, and any man who didn't want to be there when that happened was a coward.

By the end of September, the German forces realized that they were being defeated and soon the war would be over. They could no longer continue the battle due to shortages of men and supplies, and it was rumoured that many German soldiers began to question

The Gillespie Memorial, Comber.

what they were fighting for. The devastation that surrounded them on a daily basis was becoming too much. Many men were fortunate to have survived this long, but the daily torment from their living conditions and seeing death all around them took its toll, both physically and mentally.

As the winter months came around for yet another year, the decision was made to light only four street lamps in Comber. The lamps that would be lit would be on certain street corners to prevent any collisions.

On 19 September, Sam Geddis was killed in action. The 2nd Presbyterian Church held an emotional memorial service for the fallen soldier after he was buried in France. Before he had joined the fight, Geddis had been a Sunday school teacher in the church and a member of the choir. He was also well-known within the legal profession as he was a clerk with Messrs Moorland and Wood in Belfast. His fiancée, Jeannie McBurney, had already lost two of her brothers in the fighting. Jeannie was left heartbroken and never married after Sam's death.

In the previous years, the women of Newtownards had argued about how big their personal sacrifice had been and how many men they had given to the armed forces. It turned out that the women of Newtownards had not given as many men as they believed; it was the women of Comber who had given more. There was no other town, apart from Lurgan, that had sent so many men to the fight. This fact was revealed at a recruitment meeting held in The Square in Comber town centre. A military band played while Captain Tait encouraged any men who were between 18 and 33 years of age to join the forces. People believed that the blood of Gillespie (Sir Robert 'Rollo' Gillespie, a legendary soldier known as 'the Strongest Man of Comber') still flowed through the veins of the men of Comber. De Wind Drive in Comber was not the only street in the town that was to be named after a fallen soldier. Captain James George Bruce was the son of Samuel Bruce, the owner of Comber Distilleries. Captain

Postcard of Comber distillery.

Bruce was killed in action on 2 October and Bruce Avenue was named after him as a memorial.

Sergeant Samuel Scott was from Newtownards but had moved to Canada prior to the Great War. On the outbreak of war he enlisted in Canada and served at the front with the Canadian Field Artillery. Unlike so many others, Scott was able to die at home with his loved ones by his side. He had caught influenza and was sent back to his home in Canada to be with his wife and children.

Armistice

After more than four years of fighting, countless lives had been lost. It had finally become clear to the German forces in late October and early November that the allies were going to win. The newly formed Royal Air Force (RAF) had been highly successful in gaining information about the enemy positions. Once the allied forces were able to breach the German Siegfried Line on 29 September, the outcome of the war was set. Marshal Foch received an armistice delegation on 8 November and the Germans were given seventy-two hours in which to agree to the terms. Kaiser Wilhelm abdicated on 9 November and the terms for armistice were agreed. On 11 November, the armistice was signed at 5.00 am and came into effect at 11.00 am. As soon as the clocks struck 11.00 am, everyone was to lay down their arms and the fighting was to end immediately. Once the terms had been agreed and the conflict was finally going to end, messengers were quickly dispatched to the front. In some parts of the trenches the fighting stopped on both sides as soon as the message had been received. In other places the fighting and deaths continued up to the last seconds before the clock struck 11.00 am.

At 11.00 am, the guns at the front fell silent. For a moment afterwards, nobody knew quite what to do. After the conflict, many men were afraid to climb out of the trenches in case the enemy was planning one final attack. Slowly, men crept out of the trenches and began to leave. By the end of the day, the towns along the front lines had filled with men from both sides. For the first time in years these men could relax. The drinks flowed as the troops danced in the streets of the towns with the locals. In the days that followed, men who had been stranded away from their units crept into the towns and would learn that the war was over. There were stories of men who made their way into the nearest towns and were greeted by groups of German soldiers. Despite having been fighting each other for more than four years, there was no hostility between the men. They greeted each other like old friends, hugged and celebrated the end of the war. The allied forces did not stop serving the people after the guns had fallen silent. As the German forces began to withdraw, British troops searched through the bombed streets for soldiers and civilians who were injured and trapped.

Aftermath for the town

When the men returned home, many of them had been left disabled. Many of those who returned were suffering from shellshock. This mental disorder, now known as post-traumatic stress disorder (PTSD), greatly affected many of the men. For the physically injured soldier, there was the Incorporated Cripples' Guild. This was the only institute in Ireland which assisted 'cripples' over the age of 14 with training to return to work.

The Old Priory. This sits opposite the site that would later become the war memorial.

Although there were many fallen soldiers from the town, none of those deaths was due to being shot for desertion or disobedience. The official end date of the war was not until the summer of 1921 and any serviceman who died up until this time was considered a casualty of war. More than 800 men lost their lives during this period. On 14 November, a united service was held in the 1st Comber Presbyterian Church to give thanks for the end of the war. The only church representative who didn't attend was Reverend McConnell as he was suffering from influenza. The choirs sang hymns and a collection was taken for the Red Cross. During the run-up to Christmas, there was an outpouring of charity for the troops. All this came at a time when a wave of the so-called Spanish flu pandemic struck the town. Annie Taylor lost her husband and three of her sons during this outbreak.

Aftermath for Ireland

Edward Carson continued to be politically active in Ulster until he was offered the position of the first prime minister. However, he had no desire to take the position and pleaded ill health. When he stepped down as leader of the Ulster Unionist Party he urged his followers to ensure that the Catholic minority had nothing to fear from the Protestant majority. The Newtownards Teachers' Association had its annual meeting in November and took the opportunity to thank Edward Carson for his help with the questions that hung over primary education in Ireland. James Craig, who had played a large part in mobilizing the Ulster Unionist resistance during the Home Rule crisis before the war, became prime minister of Northern Ireland in 1921. In taking the position he sacrificed a promising political career in London. Not only was he the first prime minister of the country, he held the position until his death.

As soon as the guns had fallen silent, the town began the task of ensuring that Unionism was brought back to the forefront of the political agenda. On 12 November, the town held a meeting to choose who would represent North Down in Parliament. Mr T.C. Brown was selected to be the next candidate and Mr Crawford was selected as chairman of the committee. There was debate regarding who should be president and the issues that faced Ulster now that the war was over and the country was to be divided.

Orange Order, 12 July 1919.

Stormont under construction in 1928.

Stormont from above.

Memorials

It would be some time before the first war memorials were erected
for the fallen. The first war memorial stone was placed in the outer
wall of Greyabbey Parish Church of Ireland on 2 April 1921. A war
memorial was not erected in Newtownards until May 1934, sixteen
years after the conflict had ended. The delay was caused by several
public meetings which postponed any plans for a memorial. There
were several suggestions including a public park, public baths and
a terrace of houses for war widows and children, but every plan
was postponed due to lack of funds.

While snow was falling on the ground in March 1924, a group
of ex-servicemen took to the grounds outside the Priory and built
a memorial. A single snowman stood proudly in the town that
day on the bowling green. The following year, a concert was held
to raise funds for a permanent memorial while a temporary one

was placed in Conway Square for those who died at the Battle of the Somme. In Victoria Avenue, in the grounds of the Royal British Legion, there had been a temporary memorial for several years while a decision was made regarding a permanent structure. This was the beginning of memorials appearing across the country for the fallen.

In 1933, a temporary memorial was placed on the bowling green where the snowman once stood. While everyone debated this temporary memorial and thought about how the present

James Craig.

one should look, Mr R.P. Dorrian was collecting the names of the fallen soldiers from the town. The *Newtownards Chronicle* published two lists in September 1933 with the names of soldiers who had died. It was hoped that any mistakes or forgotten names would be spotted by the families and could be changed. When the memorial was finally unveiled by the Marquis of Londonderry, it was a sight to behold. A giant Mourne granite obelisk was placed in the same spot where the snowman from years before had stood, with the names of the fallen soldiers engraved for all to see. At the beginning of the war, there were fifteen Irish regiments within the British army. The numbers of servicemen ranged from 25,000 to 30,000 men.

As the menfolk recovered from the war, the women found solace in their work. By the end of the conflict there were 1.3 million more women in employment than there had been in 1914. However, now that their men were returning from the armed forces, the women were displaced in order to give jobs back to the men. Many of the women who could embroider had the opportunity to increase their income. Linen agents contacted women to embroider designs on handkerchiefs. When the opportunity of 'initialling' was available, the women would rush to the local agent in the hope of getting the job, as initialling paid a lot more than embroidering flowers. The linen industry in Ireland had received around £11 million of investment throughout the war years as it was the mills in Comber that had provided the linen to cover the fighter planes for the RAF.

Field Marshal Lord French often stated that 'the war was won on Ulster wings' as the effort from the mills was widely recognized.

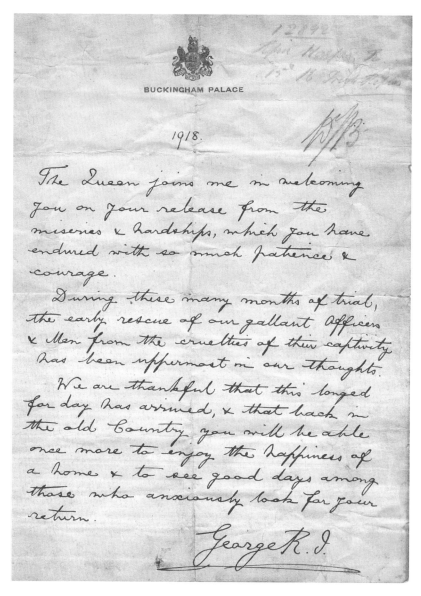

Letter from King George V in 1918.

Comber war memorial unveiled on 14 April 1923.

Comber memorial.

Snowman for the Fallen

Index

10th (Irish) Division, 108
36th (Ulster) Division, 31, 39, 49, 86, 88–9, 108

Asquith, Herbert (Prime Minister), 30
Audacious, 43–5

Baden-Powell (Lord), 69
Ballygowan, 5
Ballyhalbert, 105, 113
Ballywalter, 22
Bangor, 23, 39, 49, 80, 110
Belfast, 1, 5, 26, 35–6, 44, 57, 62, 68–9, 71, 77, 83, 89, 92–3, 98, 107–109, 117, 120, 122, 124
Belgian Prince, 110, 124
Benny Spiro, 25
Boy Scouts, 69, 77, 106
Boyne, Battle of, 29, 86

Carpathia, RMS, 122
Carson, Edward, 15, 17–22, 31, 49, 64, 109, 130
Castle Gardens, 22
Catholic, 7–8, 12, 130
Civil War, 7, 56, 84, 102
Clandeboye, 23, 39, 56, 88–9, 122
Comber, 5, 22, 47, 49, 98, 106, 111–13, 118, 120–2, 124, 126–7, 130, 133
Comber Railway, 98, 122
Comber Whiskey, 5, 75, 107–108, 127
Comfort Committee, 47, 58
Concentration Camp, 36, 83
Conlig, 23

Conway Square, 22, 125, 133
Coronel, Battle of, 45
County Down, 1, 5, 7, 28, 84, 89, 106, 110, 116
Crawford, Major Frederick, 25

Distinguished Conduct Medal, 71
Dixon Family, 37, 68, 104, 116
Donaghadee, 5, 22, 26–7, 45, 71, 80, 89, 98
Dublin, 71, 82–4, 92, 107, 124
Dunleath, Lord, 22, 27, 103

Easter Rising, 81–4, 99, 116
Espionage, 31–7

Ferdinand, Archduke Franz, 30
Flush Hall, 52–5

Greyabbey, 5, 122, 132
Gun running, 24–30, 50, 107
Guns, 17, 49

Harland and Wolff, 62, 89, 93
Home Rule, 7, 10–16, 18, 20–2, 25, 49, 51, 73, 84, 107, 116, 130

Irish Republican Army (IRA), 107
Irish Republican Brotherhood (The Brotherhood), 81–2
Irish Sea, 44, 60, 77, 95, 105, 114
Isle of Man, 36, 60

King George, 12, 110
Kitchener, Lord, 30, 39, 85–6, 104
Kitchener's Army, 60

Lewis, C.S., 120
Londonderry, Marchioness of, 97
Londonderry, Marquis of, 51, 124, 133
Lusitania, RMS, 61–2, 104

Mayne, 28, 50, 52
Messines, Battle of, 108
Military Cross, 90
Military Medal, 84, 86, 89, 103
Mount Pleasant, 28, 50, 52
Mount Stewart, 124–5
Movilla Abbey, 1, 77

Nationalist, 17, 49, 107, 116
Neuve Chapelle, Battle of, 58–60, 64, 78, 80
Newry, 5, 55
Newtownards Chronicle, 14, 22, 32, 35–6, 64, 78, 133

Olympic Liner, 43, 45, 62, 93
Orangemen, 29
Orange Order, 15–16, 29, 64, 84, 86–7
Orlock Hill, 69

Portaferry, 95, 106, 122, 125
Prohibition, 61, 75
Protestant, 7–8, 130

Quinn, Willie, 52–5

Red Cross, 68, 98, 104, 130
Relief Fund, 47, 68
Roses, 37, 66, 68, 104, 116
Royal Inniskilling Fusiliers, 39
Royal Irish Fusiliers, 39, 111
Royal Irish Rifles, 39, 59–60, 66, 71, 77, 88–90, 103, 109, 111, 119

Scandal, 67, 99
Scarlet Fever, 40–2,
Scrabo Hill, 1, 36, 52,
Sinn Fein, 107, 116
Somme, Battle of, 86–91, 103, 105, 108–109, 111, 133
Strangford Lough, 1, 60, 81, 95
Suffragists, 56–7

Titanic, RMS, 43, 89, 93, 122

U-Boat, 85, 61–2, 85, 94–5, 104–105, 110–11, 113, 122–3
Ulster Print Works, 54
Ulster Province, 1, 7, 10, 14, 16–18, 20–2, 26, 29, 31, 39, 52, 56–7, 73, 81, 116, 118, 124–5, 130
Ulster Volunteer Force (UVF), 15–22, 24–9, 30–1, 39, 49–51, 56, 68, 84–5, 107
Ulster Women's Unionist Council, 56
Unionism, 8, 15, 130
Unionist, 5, 7, 12, 15, 20–1, 25, 52, 64, 81, 107, 130
UVF Nursing Corps, 56, 68
Victoria Cross, 118

White Star Liner, 43
Whitespots, 31–2, 36
Wilde, Oscar, 15
Women's Auxiliary Corps, 99
Women's Land Army, 115